C I T Y P A C K

San Francisco

By Mick Sinclair

2ND EDITION

Fodor's Travel Publications, Inc.
New York • Toronto • London • Sydney • Auckland

WWW.FODORS.COM/

Contents

About this book

Citypack San Francisco is divided into six sections to cover the six most important aspects of your visit to San Francisco. It includes:

- The author's view of the city and its people
- Itineraries, walks and excursions
- The top 25 sights to visit—as selected by the author
- Features on what makes the city special
- Detailed listings of restaurants, hotels, shops and nightlife
- Practical information

In addition, easy-to-read side panels provide extra facts and snippets, highlights of places to visit, and invaluable practical advice.

CROSS-REFERENCES

To help you make the most of your visit, cross-references, indicated by ▶ , show you where to find additional information about a place or subject.

MAPS

- **The fold-out map** in the wallet at the back of the book is a comprehensive street plan of San Francisco. All the map references given in the book refer to this map. For example, the Asian Art Museum, in Golden Gate Park, has the following information: ✚ E7—indicating the grid square in which the Asian Art Museum will be found.
- **The city-center maps** found on the inside front and back covers of the book itself are for quick reference. They show the Top 25 Sights, described on pages 24–48, which are clearly plotted by number (1 – 25, not page number) from west to east across the city.

PRICES

Where appropriate, an indication of the cost of an establishment is given by $ signs: **$$$** denotes higher prices, **$$** denotes average prices, while **$** denotes lower charges.

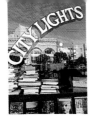

SAN FRANCISCO *life*

INTRODUCING SAN FRANCISCO

Carnival in the Mission District

The "F" word

The worst mistake a newcomer to San Francisco is likely to make is not stumbling into a threatening neighborhood but calling the city "Frisco," a term known locally as the "F word." Visitors can, however, earn themselves considerable respect by adopting the habit, which extends across all of northern California, of referring to San Francisco simply as "the city."

Since the 1850s Gold Rush transformed it from a hamlet into a city, San Francisco has been different from the rest. The anything-goes atmosphere helped to create a tolerant city that thrives on change. San Francisco has frequently set the nation's cultural and social pace—witnessing the birth of 1950s Beats, of 1960s hippies, of 1970s gay and lesbian liberation—and is currently vibrant with media and software companies alert to the global information revolution; computer-dominated "Silicon Valley" is just an hour's drive away. As California approaches the 21st century, the state is set to become the first in the United States without an ethnic majority. San Francisco, home to a multitude of races, religions and cultures, is a symbol of this multiculturalism.

Besides its cosmopolitanism, San Francisco is also full of quickly revealed idiosyncrasies. Cable cars, steep streets, morning fogs, and intricate Victorian architecture are all part of San Francisco's character and help fuel the pride that the majority of its residents feel, as does the proliferation of cafés, where smoking may be frowned upon but coffee is regarded as the elixir of life.

With 18 million annual arrivals, San Francisco is the most visited city in the United States and tourism has been its major source of income since the 1970s. As a result, the city is noticeably visitor-friendly: information is easily accessed and opportunities to explore beneath the surface are plentiful.

Geography has done San Francisco many favors, most obviously in that the city occupies a peninsula that is scenically spectacular and that prevents the onset of urban sprawl. Instead, the city is compact and divides into a network of neighborhoods, all linked by public transportation.

Geology has been less benevolent, with several major fault lines close to the city. An earthquake destroyed San Francisco completely in 1906, another inflicted serious damage in 1989, and a major quake could strike at any time. Visitors might take solace in the statistical unlikelihood of this occurring during their stay and the fact that San Francisco is among the world leaders in earthquake preparedness: basic precautions are even suggested in the city phone book.

Buses

San Francisco is easy to travel around by bus, but actual bus numbers can be confusing. Throughout this book, we indicate the numbered bus routes passing by or close to a particular site, though the city's one-way system causes buses to follow slightly different outbound and inbound routes.

A mural in the Mission District illustrates the multicultural nature of San Francisco's population

SAN FRANCISCO IN FIGURES

DISTANCES	Distance from New York: 2,930 miles Distance from Los Angeles: 397 miles Distance from London: 6,010 miles Distance from Berlin: 6,094 miles
SIZE	Population: 724,000; 14th largest city in U.S.A. Area: 46.38 square miles Miles of waterfront: 7.5 Miles of shoreline: 8.4
GEOGRAPHY	Latitude: N 37° 46' 39" Longitude: W 122° 24' 40" Foundation: sandstone, shale, volcanic rock Highest point: Mt. Davidson, 938 feet Lowest point: sea level Hills: 43 Islands within city limits: 11 Park acreage within city limits: 8,100
HISTORY	Founded: Presidio of San Francisco, September 17, 1776 Oldest structure: Mission Dolores, 1791 Population at first census, 1798: 627
STREETS OF SAN FRANCISCO	Longest street: Mission Street Widest street: Van Ness Avenue Steepest streets: Filbert between Leavenworth and Hyde, and 22nd Street between Church and Vicksburg, both with 31.5 percent gradients
SYMBOLS	City flag: a Phoenix rising from the ashes on a white background bordered by gold Official flower: dahlia Official song: *San Francisco* Official ballad: *I Left My Heart in San Francisco* Official motto: *Oro en paz, Fierro en guerra* ("Gold in peace, Iron in war")
WEATHER	Wettest month: January, 4.48 inches Driest month: July, 0.04 inches Warmest month: September, mean maximum 68.9 °F Coolest month: January, mean maximum 56.1 °F Annual mean temperatures: high 62.5 °F; low 51 °F

SAN FRANCISCO PEOPLE

FRANCIS FORD COPPOLA
Detroit-born Francis Ford Coppola rose to prominence as director of *The Godfather*. He located his independent Zoetrope film company in San Francisco during the 1970s, and it was his money that saved the flatiron-style Columbus Tower from demolition. Coppola is frequently to be seen in and around North Beach restaurants.

DIANNE FEINSTEIN
Feinstein became city mayor through the assassination of the incumbent in 1978 and defied expectations by winning the two subsequent mayoral elections. Having raised the profile of women in city politics and given a platform to sexual minority groups, Feinstein was elected to represent California in the U.S. Senate.

LAWRENCE FERLINGHETTI
Ferlinghetti's poetry helped to make him one of the leading figures of the 1950s Beat Generation, as did his co-ownership of the City Lights bookstore, the country's first exclusively paperback bookshop, which published, to great controversy, Allen Ginsberg's seminal *Howl* in 1956.

ARMISTEAD MAUPIN
Beginning as a column in the *San Francisco Chronicle*, Armistead Maupin's *Tales of the City*—a saga of the ups and downs of a group of typically untypical 1970s San Franciscans—evolved into novels and a TV series. A gay man from the US's conservative deep South, Maupin is a respected commentator on San Francisco life.

DAVID SMITH
As an idealistic medical student, Smith founded the Haight-Ashbury Free Clinic during 1967 when San Francisco's hippie population was poorly served by established medical facilities. Smith's free clinics grew in number and now operate from 20 sites around the Bay Area, serving an average of 800 low-income patients a day.

Francis Ford Coppola

The Grateful Dead
Formed in the mid-1960s to play LSD-influenced R&B music for hours at a time to the residents of Haight-Ashbury, the Grateful Dead were among the original psychedelic rock bands that helped to make San Francisco the heart of the hippie movement. They continued to be enormously popular for three decades, still cherishing their original idealistic beliefs, but the death in 1995 of lead guitarist Jerry Garcia drew to an end this chapter in San Francisco's musical life.

A CHRONOLOGY

Pre-1776	An estimated 13,000 Native Americans live on either side of the Golden Gate
1776	Traveling from their Californian base at Monterey, the Spanish build a *presidio* (or garrison) and mission on the northern tip of the San Francisco peninsula
1821	Newly independent Mexico acquires California from Spain
1846	U.S.A. takes control of California
1848	Gold is discovered near Sacramento, 87 miles northeast of San Francisco
1849	The California Gold Rush begins. San Francisco's population soars from 812 to 20,000
1851	San Francisco becomes the fourth-busiest port in the United States
1853	An attempt to corner the rice market leads to the bankruptcy of entrepreneur Joshua Norton, who assumes a new identity as Emperor Norton and becomes a celebrated eccentric
1873	The city's first cable car runs along Clay Street
1906	On April 18 a major earthquake (8.3 on the Richter Scale) followed by a three-day fire leaves 3,000 dead and destroys 28,000 buildings
1915	The Panama Pacific Exposition symbolizes the city's recovery from the earthquake
1934	Police fatally shoot two striking dockers and 150,000 people join a four-day general strike in protest
1936	Bay Bridge is completed
1937	Golden Gate Bridge is completed
1941	U.S. entry into World War II stimulates war industries and brings an influx of military and

civilian personnel to the city. Employment in
the shipyards grows from 4,000 to 260,000

1945 The United Nations charter is signed by 50
countries in the San Francisco Opera House;
the Soviet Union vetoes a proposal to make
San Francisco the U.N.'s permanent home

1957 Publication of Allen Ginsberg's poem *Howl* by
North Beach bookstore-publisher City Lights
helps the neighborhood become the center of
an influx of what *San Francisco Chronicle*
columnist Herb Caen (▶ 12) labels "beatniks"

1964 Students at Berkeley form the nonviolent
Free Speech Movement and instigate the first
of the campus revolts that spread across the
country in succeeding years

1966 The militant African-American group, the
Black Panthers, forms in Oakland

1967 The "Summer of Love:" Young people arrive
from across the country and Haight-Ashbury's
hippie population grows from 7,000 to 75,000

1977 Harvey Milk becomes the nation's first openly
gay candidate to be elected to public office

1978 Harvey Milk and Mayor George Moscone are
assassinated at City Hall by a former city
politician, Dan White

1979 The lightweight five-year prison sentence
bestowed on White prompts the "White Night
Riot" when predominantly gay demonstrators
marched on City Hall, causing $1 million worth
of damage

1989 The Loma Prieta earthquake (7.1 on the
Richter scale) kills 67 people and closes the
Bay Bridge for a month

1991 Fires rage across the Oakland Hills on the east
side of San Francisco Bay, killing 25 and
destroying 3,000 homes

PEOPLE & EVENTS FROM HISTORY

The Big Four

The so-called Big Four—Charles Crocker, Mark Hopkins, Collis P. Huntington, and Leland Stanford—were Gold-Rush shopkeepers who joined forces in 1865 to form the Southern Pacific Railroad. This was the first transcontinental railroad and the enterprise not only earned fortunes for the Big Four but also fueled a corrupt business empire that dominated San Franciscan life for decades.

The 1906 earthquake and fire

The earthquake that struck at 5:12AM on April 18, 1906, a product of the San Andreas Fault, caused relatively minor damage in itself but by rupturing gas and water mains it enabled fires to break out and burn uncontrolled. The fires eventually left 3,000 acres of San Francisco devastated, and rendered 250,000 of the city's 400,000 inhabitants homeless.

HERB CAEN

His byline appearing in the *San Francisco Chronicle* since 1938, Herb Caen was the city's most widely read columnist until his death in February 1997. Whether describing city politics or the latest in-vogue restaurant, Caen's love of San Francisco and awareness of its traditions never failed to shine through his prose. A judge once described Caen as the "journalistic equivalent of the Golden Gate Bridge."

LILLIE COIT

Raised for high society, Lillie Coit outraged her peers by wearing men's clothes, playing poker with dockers, smoking cigars, and taking a special interest in San Francisco's volunteer fire brigades. When she died in 1929, Lillie left $100,000 for the beautification of the city, and it was decided to use these funds to erect a memorial—the present Coit Tower—to the city's volunteer firefighters.

JOHN MCLAREN

Born in Scotland in 1846, John McLaren migrated to California and became supervisor of Golden Gate Park. So well-known did the "tyrannical and capricious" Scot become in San Francisco that his birthday was celebrated as a civic event, and a special law was passed in 1917 enabling him to work beyond retirement age. McLaren continued as park supervisor until his death in 1943.

Coit Tower, erected as a memorial to Lillie Coit

SAN FRANCISCO

how to organize your time

13

ITINERARIES

Steep hills notwithstanding, San Francisco is well suited to walking and has an excellent public transportation system. If your time is limited, careful planning will ensure that you get the most from this fascinating city and its environs.

ITINERARY ONE	ALCATRAZ TO TELEGRAPH HILL
Morning	Avoid the tourist crowds by taking the first ferry from Fisherman's Wharf over to the island prison of Alcatraz (➤ 38) Returning from Alcatraz, walk or take public transportation from Fisherman's Wharf to North Beach (➤ 51). Explore North Beach's cafés and bookstores, the North Beach Museum (➤ 53), Washington Square (➤ 56) and the Church of Saints Peter and Paul (➤ 52)
Lunch	Mario's Bohemian Cigar Store or Caffè Trieste (➤ 68), Basta Pasta or Fior d'Italia (➤ 65), or North Beach Pizza (➤ 63)
Afternoon	Continue to Telegraph Hill's Coit Tower (➤ 57) and the flower-lined Filbert Steps (➤ 60)
ITINERARY TWO	CHINATOWN TO FORT MASON CULTURE CENTER
Morning	Stroll through Chinatown (➤ 50), visiting the three temples of Waverly Place (➤ 60) and the neighborhood shops (➤ 76)
Lunch	Sample a Chinatown *dim sum* lunch at Pot Sticker or Royal Jade, which also has a buffet, or try the House of Nanking (➤ 64)
Afternoon	Walk or take public transportation to Russian Hill (➤ 51), stopping to visit Ina Coolbrith Park at Taylor and Vallejo Streets (➤ 56), and strolling along Green Street (➤ 60) Continue to Pacific Heights (➤ 51), walk through Lafayette Park (➤ 56), then explore the shops and restaurants of Union Street (➤ 60) Take public transportation to Fort Mason Culture Center (➤ 35), and explore the museums and galleries

ITINERARY THREE	NOB HILL TO SOMA
Morning	Start the day at Nob Hill (► 50) Tour Grace Cathedral (► 40) and look inside some of the neighborhood's exclusive hotels Walk or take public transportation to the Financial District. Visit the distinctive Transamerica Pyramid (► 45), view the 19th-century buildings of Jackson Square and the towering Bank of America HQ (► 54) Tour the Wells Fargo Museum (► 46) inside the Wells Fargo Bank
Lunch	Financial District luxury options are Aqua and Tommy Toy's (► 62); less expensive options are Yank Sing (► 64) and Café Bastille (► 68)
Afternoon	Take public transportation to SoMa (► 51) and spend the rest of the day at the San Francisco Museum of Modern Art (► 44)
Refreshment	The Compass Rose (► 69)
ITINERARY FOUR	HAIGHT-ASHBURY TO GOLDEN GATE PARK
Morning	Start the day in Haight-Ashbury (► 50) Tour some of the neighborhood's streets and browse Haight Street's unusual shops
Lunch	Haight-Ashbury's Kan Zaman or Jammin' Java (► 68)
Afternoon	Walk from Haight-Ashbury into Golden Gate Park (► 25). Visit the park's Conservatory of Flowers and continue to the M. H. De Young Memorial Museum (► 29) and Asian Art Museum (► 28). With children, allocate time for the park's California Academy of Sciences (► 30). Should the park be of more appeal than its museums, tour it by bicycle rented from one of the outlets on Stanyan Street
Refreshment	The café at the M. H. De Young Memorial Museum (► 29)

WALKS

One of the many skyscrapers of the Financial District

THE SIGHTS

- Circle Gallery (▶ 54)
- Bank of America HQ (▶ 54)
- Old St. Mary's Church (▶ 52)
- Chinese Historical Society of America (▶ 43)
- Tien Hou Temple (▶ 52)
- Transamerica Pyramid (▶ 45)

INFORMATION

Distance Approx 1½ miles
Time 2 hours
Start point Westin St. Francis Hotel, Union Square
🚇 K5
🚌 2, 3, 4, 6, 38, 71;
Powell–Hyde or
Powell–Mason cable car
End point North Beach
🚇 K3/4

UNION SQUARE TO NORTH BEACH

Begin in the lobby of the Westin St. Francis Hotel (▶ 84), where the grandfather clock has long been a renowned San Franciscan meeting place. Leave the hotel and cross Union Square. Note the square's Dewey Monument, with its bronze figure of Victory reputedly modeled on Alma Spreckels (▶ 26).

Maiden Lane and the Financial District Leave the square, crossing Stockton Street for Maiden Lane (▶ 60). On Maiden Lane, note the Circle Gallery. From Maiden Lane, walk north along Kearny Street past the Bank of America HQ and turn left onto California Street, walking uphill and crossing the street for Old St. Mary's Church.

Coffee breaks Recommended stops for coffee are Franciscan Croissant (✉ 301 Sutter Street on the corner with Grant Avenue ☎ 415/398–8276), with excellent coffee and extensive croissants and pastries; or Mocca on Maiden Lane (✉ 175 Maiden Lane ☎ 415/956–1188), which has outdoor seating and hot, filling sandwiches.

Chinatown Stroll along Grant Avenue into the heart of Chinatown. Turn onto Commercial Street and visit the Chinese Historical Society of America. Afterward return to Grant Avenue and continue on to Waverly Place (▶ 60) and the Tien Hou Temple. Turn right along Washington Street to Portsmouth Square, noting the memorial on the north side to Robert Louis Stevenson, and go straight on for a visit to the Transamerica Pyramid (▶ 45).

Time for lunch Walk, or take a bus, along Columbus Avenue for North Beach and lunch. For lunch suggestions, see Itinerary One (▶ 14).

NORTH BEACH TO THE TRANSAMERICA PYRAMID

After lunch, browse around City Lights, a bookstore pivotal to the 1950s Beat Generation. Alongside, Jack Kerouac Street was named for one of the movement's leading figures, and the adjacent Vesuvio (▶ 82) was a popular hangout. Across Columbus Avenue, note the Condor Bistro, formerly the Condor Club and, in 1964, scene of the first topless act in the United States (commemorated by a plaque).

North Beach museums and churches Cross to Stockton Street for the North Beach Museum. Return along Vallejo Street to Columbus Avenue, crossing the latter for the Church of St. Francis of Assisi, founded in 1849 and the first Catholic church in California since the Spanish missions. Continue north, browsing around Grant Avenue's unusual shops. Turn onto Union Street for Washington Square and the Church of Saints Peter and Paul. Climb Filbert Street (or use bus 39) to reach Coit Tower, then descend the Filbert Steps. In Montgomery Street, note the art deco apartment building at number 1360, which was featured, with Humphrey Bogart and Lauren Bacall, in the 1947 film *Dark Passage.* Follow Montgomery Street south to return to North Beach.

THE SIGHTS

- City Lights bookstore (▶ 73)
- North Beach Museum (▶ 53)
- Washington Square (▶ 56)
- Church of Saints Peter and Paul (▶ 52)
- Coit Tower (▶ 57)
- Filbert Steps (▶ 60)

INFORMATION

Distance 1¼ miles
Time 1½–2 hours
Start point City Lights bookstore
🚇 K4
🚌 15, 41, 83
End point Montgomery Street
🚌 L4

More Beat landmarks

Devotees of the 1950s Beat Generation might like to extend their walk to include 1010 Montgomery Street, Allen Ginsberg's home when he completed *Howl*. Ginsberg read the poem in public for the first time at 3119 Filmore Street, in Pacific Heights. Jack Kerouac, meanwhile, wrote parts of *On The Road* in the loft of 29 Russell Street, in Russian Hill.

Vesuvio bar and café

EVENING STROLLS

San Francisco offers you a number of alluring possibilities for enjoying a pre-dinner tipple in interesting surroundings before taking a short, appetite-sharpening stroll to a restaurant.

The view from the Carnelian Room, on the 52nd floor of the Bank of America HQ

THE CARNELIAN ROOM & NORTH BEACH OR CHINATOWN

Start the evening with a drink at the Carnelian Room (➤ 81), enjoying the view from this 52nd floor of the Bank of America HQ (➤ 54). Afterwards, walk north into Chinatown or North Beach for dinner.

COIT TOWER & NORTH BEACH OR CHINATOWN

Take the bus or climb the hill leading to Coit Tower (➤ 57; open until 7:30PM in summer, otherwise closing at 6) for a view across the city at twilight. Walk down the hill for dinner in North Beach or Chinatown.

THE CLIFT & UNION SQUARE

Relax with a cocktail amid the artworks in the art deco Redwood Room of The Clift hotel (➤ 81) before strolling into the Union Square area for dinner.

THE MARRIOTT & SOMA OR UNION SQUARE

Escape the sight of what many San Franciscans consider a blight on the skyline by stepping inside the Marriott Hotel (➤ 54) for a drink at the 39th-floor View Lounge. Afterwards, walk into SoMa or the Union Square area for dinner.

ORGANIZED SIGHTSEEING

WALKING TOURS

City Guides (☎ 415/557–4266) operate free daily tours, including City Hall, Victorian-era Haight-Ashbury, Nob Hill, Sutro Heights Park, the mansions of Pacific Heights, and the murals of the Mission District.

The Wok Wiz (☎ 415/355–9657) operate popular tours that offer a three-hour introduction to Chinatown, visiting herb shops, artists, and historic sites, with an optional lunch that unravels the mysteries of *dim sum*.

Cruisin' the Castro (☎ 415/550–8110) tours, giving an excellent two-hour outline of San Francisco's gay and lesbian past, take place in the Castro district.

Helen's Walk Tour (☎ 510/524–4544) gives participants a choice of themes and areas, but is memorable above all for the infectious enthusiasm of the guide herself.

BOAT RIDES

Red & White Fleet (☎ 800/229–2784) operate a 45-minute narrated cruise on San Francisco Bay, circling Alcatraz and Angel Island and passing beneath the Golden Gate Bridge.

Blue & Gold Fleet (☎ 415/705–5444) offer a similar narrated bay voyage, but one that lasts 75 minutes and passes under the Bay Bridge as well as the Golden Gate Bridge.

BUS TOURS

If your time is very limited, a guided bus tour is one way to see the city highlights quickly. **Tower Tours** (☎ 415/434–TOUR) have a half-day tour of the city, which can be combined with a cruise on the bay.

Gray Line Tours (☎ 415/558–9400) offer both a half-day tour and an evening tour that includes a walk around Chinatown and an optional dinner.

Air tours

For an overview of the city, San Francisco Helicopter Tours (☎ 800/400–2404) offer half-hour flights revealing the natural drama of the city and of San Francisco Bay from above. Prices start at $70.

On the evening ferry to Sausalito

EXCURSIONS

INFORMATION

Berkeley & Oakland

☎ BART information:
510/992–2278. Berkeley
Campus information:
510/642–INFO. Oakland
Convention & Visitors
Bureau: 510/839–9000.
Oakland–San Francisco
ferry Blue & Gold Fleet:
510/552–3300

▣ Berkeley: Berkeley.
Oakland: Lake Merritt for
the museum and 12th Street
for Chinatown

Sausalito & Tiburon

☎ Golden Gate Ferries:
415/923–2000.
Red & White Fleet:
800/229–2784

BERKELEY & OAKLAND

Take BART to Berkeley. Walk to Berkeley campus (► 48) and explore its museums and public buildings. From the campus, cross onto Telegraph Avenue for lively restaurants and bookstores. Continue by BART to Oakland. Tour the Oakland Museum (► 47). Walk north from the museum to look across Lake Merritt. Tour the 19th-century Camron Stanford House, beside the lake. Take BART or bus to Oakland's Chinatown and the shops and attractions of Jack London Square. Return to San Francisco by ferry for a dramatic view of the city's skyline.

SAUSALITO & TIBURON

Take a ferry from the Ferry Building or from Fisherman's Wharf to Sausalito and explore its downtown. Climb one of the hillside lanes for a view across the bay to San Francisco. Walk along Bridgeway to see the waterside homes and houseboats. Continue on foot, or take the bus, along Bridgeway for the Bay Model, a large, detailed scale model of San Francisco Bay's waterways.

Continue by ferry from Sausalito to Tiburon. Explore the shops and galleries in the wood-framed buildings and the converted houseboats of Ark Row. In summer, take the ferry from Tiburon to Angel Island State Park and explore the many bicycle and foot trails.

The waterfront at Sausalito

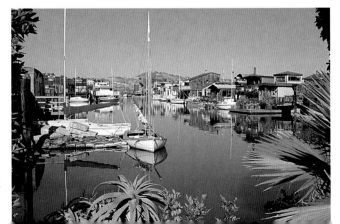

THE NORTHERN COAST

Drive across the Golden Gate Bridge and head north on Highway 1, passing Muir Beach and Stinson Beach for the Audubon Canyon Ranch, where foot trails are open for birdwatchers from mid-March to July. Continue north around Bolinas Lagoon, reaching the village of Bolinas and the tidepools of Duxbury Point. Go on to Point Reyes National Seashore, land shaped by the geological upheavals of the San Andreas Fault. Returning south, take the Panoramic Highway into Mount Tamalpais State Park. Continue to the summit of Mount Tamalpais for a view across the bay toward the city.

INFORMATION

The Northern Coast
☎ Audubon Canyon Ranch:
414/868–9244.
Point Reyes National
Seashore Ranger Station:
415/663–1092

Sonoma Wine and Visitors Center holds extensive information on the many wineries of Sonoma County

SONOMA VALLEY

Drive across the Golden Gate Bridge and continue north on Highway 101, passing through San Rafael for the town of Sonoma. Explore the Sonoma Mission and the other restored historic buildings and shops around Sonoma Plaza. Continue to the Buena Vista Winery, then head north to the hamlet of Glen Ellen and tour Jack London State Historic Park, former home of the writer whose name it bears. Continue north for Kenwood and a selection of wineries, such as Château St. Jean. Return to Sonoma and turn west along Highway 116 for Petaluma Adobe State Historic Park.

Sonoma Valley
☎ Buena Vista Winery:
707/938–1266.
Jack London State Historic
Park: 707/938–5216.
Château St. Jean:
707/833–4134.
Petaluma Adobe State
Historic Park:
707/762–4871

Major car rental companies
Avis ☎ 800/331–1212
Budget ☎ 800/601–5385
Dollar ☎ 800/800–4000
Hertz ☎ 800/654–3131

21

WHAT'S ON

Barely a week goes by without a festival of some kind being celebrated in San Francisco. The Visitor Information Center (☎ 415/391–2000), on the lower level of Hallidie Plaza, junction of Market and Powell Streets (🕐 Mon–Fri 9–5:30; Sat 9–3; Sun 10–2), has an Events Hotline: ☎ 415/391–2001 (English); 415/391–2004 (German). The *San Francisco Bay Guardian* and *SF Weekly*, and the Datebook section of the Sunday *San Francisco Chronicle* and *San Francisco Examiner* all carry details of imminent happenings. The following are selected highlights.

JANUARY / FEBRUARY	*Chinese New Year*: two weeks of Chinatown festivities; date depends on the lunar cycle
MARCH	*St. Patrick's Day* (Mar 17): Irish and would-be-Irish San Franciscans dress in green for a parade along Market Street
APRIL	*Cherry Blossom Festival*: a celebration of Japanese art and culture in Japantown
MAY	*Cinco de Mayo* (May 5): Mexican celebration centered in Mission District *Bay to Breakers*: athletes and exhibitionists race from one side of the city to the other *Carnival*: Mission District fills with music, floats, and colorful costumes
JUNE	*Lesbian & Gay Freedom Day*: huge gay and lesbian march that winds from the Castro district to Civic Center Plaza
JULY	*Independence Day* (Jul 4): the national celebration is marked by fireworks and a 50-cannon salute on the northern waterfront *San Francisco Marathon*: the country's third-largest marathon includes a crossing of the Golden Gate Bridge
SEPTEMBER	*San Francisco Blues Festival* (last weekend in Sep): ➤ 79
OCTOBER	*Halloween Parade* (Oct 31): outrageous costumes are shown off along Castro Street
NOVEMBER	*Day of the Dead* (Nov 2): Mexican tribute to the spirit world includes a macabre art exhibition and a parade through the Mission District

SAN FRANCISCO's
top 25 sights

The sights are shown on the maps on the inside front cover and inside back cover, numbered **1–25** *from west to east across the city*

1

GOLDEN GATE NRA

HIGHLIGHTS

- Coastal trail
- China Beach
- Baker Beach
- Fort Point
- Seal Rocks
- Fort Funston
- Marin Headlands
- Point Bonita Lighthouse
- Ocean Beach
- Golden Gate Promenade

INFORMATION

- ➕ A–J1–10 and off map
- ✉ GGNRA Headquarters: Building 201, Fort Mason Culture Center
- ☎ Cliff House Visitor Center (➕ A6): 415/556–8642
- 🕐 Daylight hours only recommended. Visitor Center: daily 10–4:30
- 🚌 5, 18, 19, 28, 29, 30, 31, 32, 38, 42, 48, 76
- ♿ Range from none to excellent according to location; for details ☎ 415/556–0560
- 🖐 Free
- ↔ Golden Gate Bridge (➤ 27), Fort Mason Culture Center (➤ 35), National Maritime Museum (➤ 53), Marina Green (➤ 56), Sutro Heights Park (➤ 57), San Francisco Zoo (➤ 58)
- ❓ Ranger-led tours

An enormous swath of mostly undeveloped land lying within the city and extending northward across the Golden Gate Bridge, the Golden Gate National Recreation Area is a wonderful reminder of how open and wild most of California is.

Creation From the cliffs of Fort Funston in the south to the hills of Marin County in the north, the Golden Gate National Recreation Area (GGNRA) bestows federal protection on a long, slender chunk of San Francisco's coastline. GGNRA's 74,000 acres, which lie in separate pockets and often lack clearly marked boundaries, were created in 1972 by the amalgamation of city parks, private land, and former military-owned areas. GGNRA's abandoned fortifications include a Civil War fort (Fort Point, which is located beneath the Golden Gate Bridge), and a massive World War II cannon at Baker Beach.

Exploration Much of GGNRA is best explored on foot. Start at the Cliff House Visitor Center, close to the sea lion-frequented Seal Rocks, and walk the blustery coastal trail that weaves through the coarsely vegetated hillsides that rise steeply above the tiny beach of Lands End and the forbidding waters of the Golden Gate. All vestiges of the city are entirely hidden until the appearance of the Golden Gate Bridge. This route also brings views of the isolated China Beach, named for the Chinese fishermen of the Gold Rush era who lived in shacks beside it. China Beach is one of the few San Francisco beaches that is safe for swimming, while the more accessible Baker Beach, where swimming is not permitted, is the perfect spot for a rest.

GOLDEN GATE PARK

Golden Gate Park is not only a massive slab of greenery holding several oustanding museums: it provides a stage from which San Francisco—and its jogging, kite-flying, roller-skating population— presents itself to the outside world.

Acres of fun Some 3 miles long and half a mile wide, Golden Gate Park is one of the world's largest urban parks. Secreted within its 1,000 acres are a polo field, a golf course, an archery range, a botanical garden, two major museums and the California Academy of Sciences, countless lakes, ponds, and waterfalls, and even a couple of windmills. Yet there is still sufficient space to become hopelessly lost—and quickly found again—around its tree-shrouded lanes and footpaths.

On foot The park is too large to cover entirely on foot but the eastern half is fine for strolling. Here you will find the redstone McLaren Lodge, former office of the park's creator and now an information center (maps are essential), and the 1878 Conservatory, with palm trees, water-lilies, and orchids flourishing in its humid interior. Also within easy reach is the Japanese Tea Garden, with azaleas, cherry trees, and a carp-filled pond linked by winding pathways. West of the Tea Garden a road encircles Stow Lake, at the center of which Strawberry Hill rises to a 400-foot summit.

One of the features of Golden Gate Park

HIGHLIGHTS

- Japanese Tea Garden
- Stow Lake

INFORMATION

- 🔛 A–F7/8
- ✉ Bordered by Great Highway, Lincoln Way, Fulton Street and Stanyan Street
- ☎ 415/666–7200
- 🕐 Always open; only daylight visiting is recommended
- 🍴 Excellent café ($) at M. H. De Young Memorial Museum; tea served at Japanese Tea Garden ($)
- 🚌 5, 7, 18, 21, 28, 29, 44, 71
- ♿ Good
- 🎫 Free
- ↔ Asian Art Museum (► 28), M. H. De Young Memorial Museum (► 29), California Academy of Sciences (► 30)
- ❓ Walking tours May–Oct (☎ 415/221–1311)

3

PALACE OF THE LEGION OF HONOR

HIGHLIGHTS

- Eiffel Tower, Seurat
- Water Lilies, Monet
- The Tribute Money, Rubens
- Saint John the Baptist, El Greco
- Thinker, Rodin
- The Shades, Rodin
- Holocaust sculpture, Segal
- Old Man and Old Woman, De la Tour
- Man With a Broken Nose, Rodin
- View of Golden Gate

INFORMATION

- ✚ B5
- ✉ Lincoln Park
- ☎ 415/750–3600.
  Recorded information:
  415/863–3330
- 🕐 Tue–Sun 9:30–5:15; first Sat of month 9:30–8:45. Closed Mon
- 🍴 Simple café ($)
- 🚻 18
- ♿ Good
- 🎟 Moderate; ticket also valid at the Asian Art Museum and M. H. De Young Memorial Museum on same day. Free second Wed of month
- ↔ Golden Gate National Recreation Area (▶ 24)
- ❓ Free tours daily

Rodin and San Francisco may seem an unlikely combination, but fans of the sculptor will enjoy a visit to the hilltop site where a building modeled on the Légion d'Honneur Museum in Paris displays many of his works amid a fine collection of European art.

Sugar money The collection in the California Palace of the Legion of Honor was started in the 1910s by Alma Spreckels, wife of millionaire San Franciscan sugar magnate, Adolph. Already passionate about European art, Alma met Rodin in Paris and began a lasting interest in his work. Her husband, meanwhile, was motivated to open an art museum through his bitter rivalry with another prominent San Franciscan family, the De Youngs, who had founded the M. H. De Young Memorial Museum (▶ 29).

The collections *The Shades* and *Thinker* stand in the grounds, and some 70 other Rodin works are inside the museum. The general galleries, meanwhile, are arranged in a chronological sequence from the medieval period to the early 20th century, with the highlights mostly from the 18th and 19th centuries. Downstairs, the Achenbach Foundation for Graphic Arts holds over 100,000 prints and some 3,000 drawings from artists as diverse as Albrecht Dürer and Georgia O'Keeffe, and selections are shown in short-term exhibitions (otherwise by appointment). Outside, beside the parking lot, be sure to see George Segal's *Holocaust* sculpture.

Rodin's Thinker

GOLDEN GATE BRIDGE

San Francisco's Golden Gate Bridge must surely be the most instantly recognizable, and the most beautiful, of all the bridges in the United States.

Artful engineering Named for the bay it crosses rather than its color, the bridge is a remarkable feat of artistry as well as engineering. The construction overcame the exceptional depth and strong currents of the Golden Gate, while the simple but inspired design allows it to sit with panache between the city and the wild hillsides of Marin County, its upper portions often evocatively shrouded in fog.

Loathed then loved A bond issue of $35 million was authorized in 1930 to finance the bridge's construction amid great antipathy from San Franciscans, many of whom feared that it would result in a loss of the natural beauty of the Golden Gate. An early design by the project's chief engineer, Joseph B. Strauss, was likened to "two grotesque steel beetles emerging from either bank." The design eventually adopted is thought to have been the work of one or more of Strauss's assistants. The affection that the bridge now enjoys among city dwellers was confirmed in 1987 when 200,000 people filed onto it to mark the 50th anniversary of its opening; their gathering caused the central span to drop by 10 feet.

Fatal attraction On a more downbeat note, the Golden Gate Bridge has become a noted spot for suicides. The first occurred three months after the bridge's opening and, to date, almost 1,000 people have ended their lives by jumping the 220 feet from the central span to the raging waters beneath, their bodies usually carried out to the Pacific by the swift currents of the bay.

DID YOU KNOW?

- Weight of steel in construction: 100,000 tons
- Length including approaches: 7 miles
- Actual bridge length: 6,450 feet
- Length of central span: 4,200 feet
- Height above water: 220 feet at low tide
- Height of towers: 746 feet
- Length of cables: 80,000 miles
- Color: International Orange, the color most easily distinguishable in fog
- Gallons of paint used annually: 5,000
- Annual vehicle crossings: 42,000,000

INFORMATION

- D1–3
- 415/921–5858
- Open to pedestrians daily 5–9
- 28, 29, 76
- Good at observation platform
- Free for pedestrians and cyclists; moderate toll for city-bound drivers
- Golden Gate National Recreation Area (► 24)
- Guided walking tours run by Roger's Custom Tours (415/742–9611)

5

ASIAN ART MUSEUM

HIGHLIGHTS

- Xuande Era blue and white porcelain
- Ming Dynasty calligraphy and fan painting
- Japanese *netsuke*
- Edo-period Japanese screen paintings
- Magnin Jade Gallery
- Tibetan *thangkas* (religious paintings)
- Tibetan thigh-bone trumpet
- Tibetan three-headed Bon figure

INFORMATION

- E7
- Golden Gate Park
- 415/668–8921. Recorded information: 415/379–8801
- Wed–Sun 10–4:45; first Wed of month 10–8:45. Closed Mon and Tue
- Excellent café ($) in M. H. De Young Memorial Museum
- 44
- Excellent
- Moderate; includes M. H. De Young Memorial Museum and Palace of the Legion of Honor if visited on same day. Free first Wed of month
- Golden Gate Park (► 25), California Academy of Sciences (► 30)
- Free tours daily. Lectures, films

It is guaranteed that something amid the wealth of treasures inside the Asian Art Museum—the largest collection of its kind in the country—will catch your eye, be it Chinese jade, Japanese netsuke *or a Tibetan thigh-bone trumpet.*

The Brundage collection The museum originated with an immense collection of Asian artifacts assembled by the industrialist and former president of the International Olympic Committee, Avery Brundage. San Francisco, with its historic and cultural links with Asia, was chosen as the site of a museum to display the Brundage acquisitions. Since its opening in 1966 the museum has expanded its stock considerably. It now has 15,000 pieces and lacks the space to show more than a fraction of the holdings at one time.

Diverse exhibits With exhibits spanning 6,000 years and diverse cultures and religions, there is a lot to be said for simply wandering through the galleries, pausing at whatever grabs your attention. The major collections are from China and include the oldest dated example of Chinese Buddhist art (A.D. 338), and important items from the Ming Dynasty (1368–1644) and Xuande Era (1426–1435). But the smaller, less obvious items can delight in equal measure, such as the wood carvings, silverwork, and textiles from Bhutan, which offer you a rare insight into this obscure country.

A carved pillar in the museum

6

M. H. DE YOUNG MEMORIAL MUSEUM

From Anatolian prayer rugs to the dresses of Yves Saint-Laurent, the M. H. De Young Memorial Museum stocks many diverse exhibits from around the world, although the fine collections of American painting and decorative art must be the main reason for a visit.

Paintings After society portraits by John Singleron Copley and his 18th-century contemporaries such as John Smibert, the paintings on display reveal the growing self-confidence of American artists and the lessening importance of European trends. By the mid-1800s, many American artists were taking inspiration from the newly settled American West: the landscapes of Albert Bierstadt and the sculpture of Frederick Remington both evoke the period's celebratory mood of expansion. Look out, too, for the entertaining room of *trompe-l'oeil* works, the most notable of the many clever canvases on display being the work of William Michael Harnett.

Furnishings The furniture collection, too, reflects America's historic shift from colony to nation, moving from English and Dutch armchairs used in New England settlements of 1670 to an elegant Federal-period parlor from 1805 Massachusetts. The flowing curves of the Queen Anne style were popular during the colonial period, but by the time of the Revolution American craftsmen had acquired the skills and creativity to evolve a new and distinctive look, adding unique rococo touches. Philadelphia emerged above Boston and New York as the center of the craft, and a grand 1780 Philadelphia high chest provides an excellent example of the period.

HIGHLIGHTS

- *Storm in the Rocky Mountains*, Bierstadt
- *A View of Donner Lake, California*, Bierstadt
- *The Ironworkers' Noontime*, Anshutz
- *Mrs. Daniel Sargent*, Copley
- *Marius Amidst the Ruins of Carthage*, Vanderlyn
- *After the Hunt*, Harnett
- *A Dinner Table at Night*, Singer Sargent
- Philadelphia high chest of drawers
- Paul Revere's silverware
- Shaker crafts

INFORMATION

- E7
- Golden Gate Park
- 415/750–3600. Recorded information: 415/863–3330
- Wed–Sun 9:30–5:15; first Wed of month 10–8:45. Closed Mon and Tue
- Excellent café ($)
- 44
- Excellent
- Moderate; includes Asian Art Museum and Palace of the Legion of Honor if visited on same day. Free first Wed of month
- Golden Gate Park (► 25), Asian Art Museum (► 28)
- Free tours daily. Lectures, films

7

CALIFORNIA ACADEMY OF SCIENCES

HIGHLIGHTS

- Splitfin flashlight fish
- Dolphins
- Safequake
- The Swamp
- Far Side of Science Gallery
- Life Through Time Gallery
- Morrison Planetarium
- Gem and Mineral Hall
- California Tidepool

INFORMATION

- ➕ E7
- ✉ Golden Gate Park
- ☎ 415/221–5100.
  Recorded information:
  415/750–7145
- 🕐 Sep–Jun daily 10–5.
  Jul–Aug daily 10–6.
  Planetarium: shows hourly
  Sat and Sun 1–4 (11–4 in
  summer); Mon–Fri 2PM.
  Laserium: shows Thu–Sun
  evenings
- 🍴 Reasonable café ($)
- 🚌 44
- ♿ Excellent
- 💲 Moderate; free first Wed
  of month
- ↔ Golden Gate Park (➤ 25),
  Asian Art Museum (➤ 28),
  M. H. De Young Memorial
  Museum (➤ 29)
- ❓ Free tours daily. Feeding
  Thu–Tue: penguins 11:30
  and 4; seals and dolphins
  every 2 hours, starting at
  10:30. Lectures, films

If you have children with you, a visit to the California Academy of Sciences can be particularly recommended as part of a day spent in Golden Gate Park, if only to experience a Californian earthquake safely.

Strange creatures Founded in 1853 by a small group of enthusiasts who held weekly meetings and published papers on the state's newly discovered animal species, the California Academy of Sciences has evolved into a sizable museum. The exhibits give a thoroughly entertaining introduction to the natural world, one that begins with a face-to-jaw encounter with a great white shark, the most imposing exhibit in a room devoted to Californian dioramas. Living creatures in the Steinhart Aquarium include alligators, dolphins, penguins, and the mysterious splitfin flashlight fish, which uses the piscine equivalent of a flashlight to find its way around very deep, very dark waters.

Hi-tech history In other galleries, a fossilized stegosaurus tail spike sits next to the computers that allow visitors to trace evolutionary links through 3.5 billion years of history. The vibrating floor of the Safequake exhibit re-creates the earthquakes that rocked San Francisco's streets in 1865 and 1906, and the Gem and Mineral Hall displays plenty of remarkable rocks, including an amethyst-lined geode and nuggets of Californian gold. The Morrison Planetarium, meanwhile, offers narrated voyages to black holes and other oddities of the cosmos, and several evenings each week stages a laserium show that creates phantasmagorical visual images to a musical accompaniment. As a final treat, allow ample time to study and enjoy the Far Side of Science Gallery, where 159 of Gary Larson's hilarious science-inspired cartoons line the walls.

8

NEPTUNE SOCIETY COLUMBARIUM

One way to convince San Franciscans that you know more about their home town than they do is to tell them about the Neptune Society Columbarium. It is among the city's most historically and architecturally noteworthy buildings, but one of which most locals are unaware.

The moving dead An elegant, three-story Victorian rotunda decorated with stained glass, the Columbarium (a final resting place for urns holding the ashes of the deceased) was designed by British architect Bernard Cahill and opened in 1898. By 1937, it stood in the heart of a 3-acre cemetery in which an estimated 10,000 people were buried. That year, however, concerns about public health resulted in cemeteries being declared illegal in San Francisco; the graves were exhumed and their contents moved out of the city.

The interior of the Columbarium

Notable niches Declared a memorial, the Columbarium itself was spared demolition but, with cremations being outlawed, it found itself without a purpose and was left to decay. Restoration of the handsome structure began in 1980, and its empty niches were once again put on sale. Guided tours focus on the architecture, but even a swift glance at the niches will reveal Eddys, Turks, and other once-illustrious families, who gave their names to city streets.

DID YOU KNOW?

- Architect: Bernard Cahill
- Year completed: 1898
- Original owners: Oddfellows Cemetery
- Owners since 1980: Neptune Society of Northern California
- Other owners: Bay City Cemeteries Association (1930), Cypress Abbey (1935)
- Number of niches: 30,000
- Number of unoccupied niches: 10,000
- Most expensive currently available niche: $56,000
- Least expensive currently available niche: $700
- Most unusual niche adornment: a set of miniature golf clubs

INFORMATION

- F6
- 1 Loraine Court
- 415/221–1838
- Daily 10–1
- 33, 38, 50
- None
- Free
- Golden Gate Park (➤ 25), Asian Art Museum (➤ 28), M. H. De Young Memorial Museum (➤ 29), California Academy of Sciences (➤ 30), Temple Emanu-El (➤ 52)
- Tours Sat 10 and 11:30

EXPLORATORIUM

HIGHLIGHTS

- Tactile Dome
- Wave Organ
- *Alien Voices*
- Sound and Hearing
- *Tornado*
- Triple Eye Lightstick
- Distorted Room
- Shadow Box
- Vision, Color, and Light
- Golden Gate Videodisc

INFORMATION

➕ G3

✉ 3601 Lyon Street

☎ 415/563–7337.
Recorded information:
415/561–0360.
Tactile Dome reservations:
415/561–0362

🕐 Sep–May Tue–Sun 10–5;
Wed 10–9:30. Jun–Aug
daily 10–6

🍴 Reasonable cafeteria ($)

🚌 28, 30

♿ Excellent

💲 Moderate; free first Wed
of month. Tactile Dome:
moderate separate fee

↔ Palace of Fine Arts (➤ 33),
Marina Green (➤ 56)

The Exploratorium is undoubtedly the best place in San Francisco to amuse young minds with low boredom thresholds, and it is no less pleasurable for adults, who will find much to engage and entertain them.

Questions and answers Founded by Frank Oppenheimer, who worked alongside his more famous brother, Robert, on the development of the atomic bomb in the 1940s, the Exploratorium occupies a single vast hall and has 650 hands-on, interactive exhibits designed to illustrate and explain the fundamentals of natural science and human perception in a user-friendly environment. Helpful red-jacketed "explainers" stroll around answering questions, and new exhibits are developed in a workshop open to public view. The odd bits of statuary you might spot gathering dust in the corners are remnants of the building's original role as part of the Palace of Fine Arts (➤ 33).

Innovative art and science Be they crackling tesla coils or coupled resonant pendulums, the exhibits stand alongside the results of an innovative artist-in-residence program: Ned Kahn's *Tornado* is a reservoir of fog continually pulled upwards in an inverted vortex, and Paul de Marinis' *Alien Voices* allows two people in separate wooden telephone booths to speak to each other in any of 16 computer-altered voices. The Golden Gate Videodisc simulates the experience of hovering above San Francisco, while the Exploratorium's most popular item (and one that requires a reservation) is the Tactile Dome, a dark space from which participants can leave only by feeling their way out on their hands and knees.

10

PALACE OF FINE ARTS

Together with the Golden Gate Bridge and City Hall, the Palace of Fine Arts is one of the most beautiful structures in San Francisco. Remarkably, it was intentionally built as a ruin and serves no practical purpose whatsoever.

Architects' playtime In 1915, ostensibly to mark the opening of the Panama Canal, San Francisco announced its recovery from the devastation of the 1906 earthquake and fire by staging the Panama Pacific International Exposition. A group of noted architects was commissioned to erect temporary structures to house the Expo on land reclaimed from the bay. One of the architects was Bernard Maybeck, and it was his Palace of Fine Arts more than any other building that captured the imagination of the Expo's 20 million visitors. Although it was intended as a temporary structure and was built mostly of plaster and chicken-wire, the Palace of Fine Arts aroused such public affection that it was preserved and then, in the 1960s, replicated in concrete at a cost of $7.5 million.

Art in ruins Maybeck designed a Roman ruin, using a classical domed rotunda as the structure's centerpiece and flanking this with a fragmented colonnade. Each group of columns was topped by weeping maidens and decorated by aimless stairways and funeral urns. The intention was to instill a sense of "moderated sadness" and to prepare visitors for the classical art exhibited in the Expo's Great Hall (now housing the Exploratorium, ► 32). Far from making one sad, however, the palace is mysterious and enchanting, an effect greatly aided by the building's reflection in the reposeful, duck-filled lagoon that lies alongside.

DID YOU KNOW?

- Architect: Bernard Maybeck
- Built: 1915
- Inspirations: Böcklin's *Isle of the Dead*; the drawings of Piranesi
- Materials: originally plaster and wood on a chicken-wire frame
- Height of rotunda: 132 feet
- Restoration begun: 1962
- Restoration completed: 1975
- Original cost: $400,000

INFORMATION

✚	G3/4
✉	3601 Lyon Street
🕐	Always open
🚌	28, 30
♿	None
💰	Free
↔	Exploratorium (► 32), Marina Green (► 56)
❓	City Guides (☎ 415/557–4266) free walking tour, usually twice monthly

11

MISSION DOLORES

Evidence of the 18th-century Spanish settlement of California rarely surfaces in today's San Francisco, but Mission Dolores, founded in 1776 and the oldest intact building in the city, provides a welcome, if modest, insight into the era.

California's missions Completed in 1791, the mission was the sixth in a chain of 21 built by the Spanish across California. From San Diego in the south to Sonoma in the north, each mission was located a day's horse-ride from the next. The Spaniards' intention was to convert Native Americans to Catholicism, to utilize their labor, and to earn their support in any colonial conflict. Mexico's independence from Spain in 1821 put the sparsely populated California in Mexican hands, and resulted in the decline and secularization of many of the missions. Most were restored under U.S. rule, many through a job-creation program that was implemented in the 1930s during the Depression.

Inside the mission Passing through the thick adobe walls, largely responsible for the mission's success in withstanding numerous earthquakes, visitors first enter the small and richly atmospheric chapel, which holds an altar dating from 1780 and is decorated with frescoes executed by Native Americans. A modest assortment of historic pieces is gathered in the mission's museum, the oldest being a baptismal register for 1776. In the mission's cemetery, headstones mark Spanish- and Mexican-era notables, while the Lourdes Grotto indicates the common grave of some 5,000 Native Americans. A door from the mission leads into the grandiose parish church, raised beside the mission in 1918 and designated a basilica by the Pope in 1952.

FORT MASON CULTURE CENTER

It is typical of San Francisco that the bleak exteriors of a set of former army barracks on the city's northern water-front now hold more than 50 diverse arts centers, theaters, galleries, and small museums.

From arms to art From the time of San Francisco's 18th-century Spanish *presidio* (or garrison) to the Korean War of the 1950s, Fort Mason served a military role. From 1972, how-ever, the troop barracks were steadily trans-formed into a vibrant cultural center that still continues to expand. A recent addition is the innovative San Francisco Museum of Modern Art Rental Gallery.

Museums The Center's small museums with their various temporary exhibitions provide the main visitor appeal. They include the African-American Historical and Cultural Center and Museo Italo-Americano, focusing on black American and Italian-American topics respec-tively, and the San Francisco Craft and Folk Art Museum. The largest and best, however, is the Mexican Museum, where space limitations result in there being only a tiny selection of 9,000 items on show, with the emphasis instead on often provocative short-term exhibitions of contemporary Hispanic art.

HIGHLIGHTS

● Mexican Museum
● San Francisco Craft and Folk Art Museum
● African American Historical and Cultural Center
● Museo Italo-Americano
● Magic Theater
● SS *Jeremiah O'Brien*
● Greens Restaurant
● Book Bay
● San Francisco Museum of Modern Art Rental Gallery
● Cowell Theater

INFORMATION

✚ H/J3
✉ Marina Boulevard at Laguna Street
☎ 415/441–5706
🕐 Individual museums vary
🍴 The excellent Greens vegetarian restaurant ($$$) and the adjoining Tassajara bakery ($)
🚌 22, 28, 30, 49
♿ Few
🎫 Individual museums free or inexpensive
↔ Golden Gate National Recreation Area (➤ 24), Hyde Street Pier Historical Ships (➤ 39), National Maritime Museum (➤ 53), Ghirardelli Square (➤ 54), Octagon House (➤ 55), Marina Green (➤ 56)
❓ Numerous special events

The San Francisco Craft and Folk Art Museum

13

ST. MARY'S CATHEDRAL

DID YOU KNOW?

- Architects: MacSweeney, Ryan and Lee
- Design consultants: Pietro Belluschi, Pier Luigi Nervi
- Year commenced: 1960
- Year completed: 1971
- Capacity: 3,900 (2,400 seated)
- Height (including cross): 266 feet
- Window dimensions: 6 feet wide by 139 feet tall

INFORMATION

- ✚ J5/6
- ✉ 1111 Gough Street
- ☎ 415/567–2020
- ⏰ Daily 6:30–5:30
- 🚌 2, 3, 4, 38
- ♿ Excellent
- 🎫 Free
- ➡ City Hall (➤ 37), Japantown (➤ 50), Lafayette Park (➤ 56)

You may see the striking modern architecture of St. Mary's Cathedral on many occasions before realizing what you are looking at, its towering, gleaming white hyperbolic paraboloids being distinctly visible from across a wide section of the city. A closer inspection should not be missed.

Undivided worship The paraboloids give the cathedral a 190-foot-high ceiling and form the shape of a Greek cross. Inside, the open-plan cathedral (formally St. Mary's Catholic Cathedral of the Assumption) can seat 2,400 people. Its design is intended to eliminate the usual divisions between a cathedral's different areas. Here, the apse, nave, transepts, baptistery, and narthex are undivided beneath the tall ceiling, in the center of which is a skylight in the shape of the Cross. The four stained-glass windows that rise from floor to ceiling in each main wall represent the four elements.

Cathedrals past The cathedral could hardly provide a greater contrast with its predecessor, now known as Old St. Mary's Church, which stands in Chinatown. Old St. Mary's opened as the first Catholic cathedral on the West Coast and served the city until 1891. In that year, a new St. Mary's took on the role until 1962, when it was destroyed by fire. Curiously, the present cathedral stands on a plot of land previously occupied by a supermarket, demolished to make way for the modernistic religious edifice.

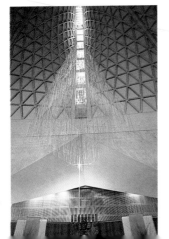

The striking interior of St. Mary's Cathedral

CITY HALL

The crowning glory of the Civic Center complex, City Hall is a beaux-arts masterpiece and seems an entirely fitting place for San Francisco to conduct its day-to-day administrative affairs.

A symbol City Hall's immense rotunda is topped by a green copper dome (modeled on St. Peter's in Rome) visible across much of the city. This intricate and inspiring building at the heart of San Francisco was completed in 1915, and arose from the drawing-boards of architects Arthur Brown and John Bakewell. Both architects studied at the École des Beaux Arts in Paris at a time when the classically inspired City Beautiful movement, which began in the 1890s, was greatly influencing American urban planning. In San Francisco, the authorities were eager for a building to symbolize San Francisco's superiority over fast-growing Los Angeles. It was Brown and Bakewell's plan—based on the French baroque style, making free use of marble and with hardly a square inch left bare of some form of decoration—that won the day. Because of earthquake damage and a restoration program, City Hall was closed to the public in the mid-1990s and its office workers moved to other buildings in the city. It is scheduled to reopen in 1998

Interior When the building is reopened to the public, it will once again be possible to go inside and climb the grand staircase—lined by ornate wrought-iron banisters and illuminated by free-standing and hanging lamps—and idle around the landings where porticoes and arches, topped by neoclassical sculptured guardians, give access to the labyrinthine complex of offices and official chambers.

DID YOU KNOW?

- Architects: Brown and Bakewell
- Prize for winning design competition: $25,000
- Building cost: $3.5 million
- Year completed: 1915
- Height of dome: 300 feet
- Occupants: mayor, elected for four-year term, and Board of Supervisors, the 11-member city legislature
- Assassination: Mayor George Moscone and Supervisor Harvey Milk, 1978
- Weddings: many, including in 1980 that of Mayor Dianne Feinstein, who invited the entire city to attend
- Previous land use: cemetery

INFORMATION

- ✚ J6
- ✉ 400 Van Ness Avenue
- ☎ 415/554-4000
- 🕐 Due to reopen after renovation in the late 1990s
- 🚌 5, 10, 20, 21, 42, 47, 49, 60, 70, 80
- Ⓜ Civic Center or Van Ness
- ♿ Good
- 🎫 Free
- ⬌ St. Mary's Cathedral (➤ 36), Levi Strauss Factory (➤ 55)

15

ALCATRAZ

As much a part of San Francisco as the Golden Gate Bridge or cable cars, the former prison of Alcatraz sits on an island in San Francisco Bay and is far and away the city's strangest sight—yet one that nobody should miss.

DID YOU KNOW?

- Named: Isla de los Alcatraces (Island of Pelicans), 1775
- Island size: 22½ acres
- Number of prisoners: 1,576
- Number of cells: 450
- Cell size: 10 feet by 4 feet

INFORMATION

- ✚ J1
- ✉ San Francisco Bay
- ☎ 415/546–2700
- 🕐 Daily, according to first and last ferries
- ⛴ Red & White Fleet from Pier 41, Fisherman's Wharf
- ♿ Few
- ✋ Moderate; advance booking advised in summer
- ❓ Self-guided audio tours recommended (moderate)

No escape A mile and a half north of Fisherman's Wharf and easily sighted from any high vantage point in the city, Alcatraz became the country's most feared place of incarceration from 1934, after the federal government took control of the island. It was turned into a top-security penitentiary for "incorrigible" criminals—those deemed beyond salvation and considered too dangerous to be held at conventional jails. There was one guard for every three inmates, work was a privilege that had to be earned through good behavior, and prisoners who did escape from their cells were faced with the prospect of crossing the freezing, swiftly moving waters of the bay (regarded as unswimmable) to freedom. Known escape attempts number 36; five escapees are unaccounted for and can perhaps be classed as successful.

Moody viewing The former cells, mess hall, hospital, and exercise yard are all open for viewing, and an audio-cassette tour with a terse commentary by former Alcatraz guards and inmates makes an excellent atmospheric accompaniment. The costs and difficulties of running an island prison, and public disquiet at the severity of the regime, contributed to Alcatraz's closure in 1963. A small museum traces the broader history of the island, which was claimed and occupied by Native Americans in 1964 for two years under an 1868 treaty that granted them rights to "unused government land."

This cell in Alcatraz was featured in the movie Escape from Alcatraz

HYDE STREET PIER HISTORICAL SHIPS

San Francisco was long the hub of the West Coast's maritime trade, and the vessels permanently docked at Hyde Street Pier, as part of the National Maritime Museum, provide an enjoyable reminder of the city's seafaring heyday and its dependence on waterborne travel before the building of the bay bridges.

Cape Horn veteran The grandest of the ships is the *Balclutha*, a steel-hulled, square-rigged ship launched in Scotland in 1886. This vessel, originally intended to carry grain between California and Europe, rounded Cape Horn several times before ending its days transporting Alaskan salmon along the West Coast. Clamber down the ladders and around the decks for a look at the restored cabins, including the elegant saloon enjoyed by the ship's master, and to scrutinize the informative explanatory texts.

Boats of the bay The 1940s cars and trucks on the lower decks of the *Eureka* suggest the era when the vessel was the world's largest passenger ferry and able to haul more than 2,000 people and 100 vehicles between San Francisco and Sausalito in a single trip. The other exhibits are the *C. A. Thayer*, built in 1895 to move the lumber used in the construction of many early Californian cities; a 1907 deep-water steam tug, *Hercules*; the *Wapama*, built in 1915 and the last survivor of 235 Californian steam schooners; a paddle-tug dating from 1914, *Eppleton Hall*, which spent its working life towing coal ships and barges in Britain; and the dainty *Alma*, a scow schooner (a type of sail-powered cargo barge) whose flat bottom enabled her to navigate with ease the shallow waters on the periphery of the bay.

HIGHLIGHTS

- *Balclutha*
- *Eureka*
- *C. A. Thayer*
- *Alma*
- *Wapama*
- *Eppleton Hall*
- *Maritime Bookstore*

INFORMATION

- ✚ J3
- ✉ Aquatic Park, foot of Hyde Street
- ☎ 415/556–3002
- 🕐 Mid-May–mid-Sep daily 10–6. Mid-Sep–mid-May daily 10–5
- 🚃 19, 32; Hyde–Powell cable car
- ♿ None
- 💲 Moderate, free on first Tue of month
- ↔ Fort Mason Culture Center (➤ 35), National Maritime Museum (➤ 53), Ghirardelli Square (➤ 54)
- ❓ Occasional ranger-led tours; periodic special events

GRACE CATHEDRAL

HIGHLIGHTS

- Ghiberti doors
- Chapel of Grace
- Stained-glass windows
- Rose window
- Gobelin tapestry

INFORMATION

- K5
- 1051 Taylor Street
- 415/749–6300
- Usually 7:30–6
- 1; California Street cable car
- Good
- Cable Car Museum (► 41), Nob Hill (► 50), Old St. Mary's Church (► 52), Huntington Park (► 56), Fairmont Hotel (► 57)
- Free tours daily, usually before and after services. Occasional lectures; exhibitions on social issues

It would be nice to think that Grace Cathedral, located as it is on the site of a former robber-baron's Nob Hill mansion, provides some spiritual atonement for the materialist excesses that characterize the neighborhood.

Slow building When the mansion of railroad boss Charles Crocker (► 12) was destroyed by the fire that followed San Francisco's 1906 earthquake, the Crocker family donated its plot to the Episcopalian church. Although the cathedral's cornerstone was laid in 1910, construction did not begin until 1928, and further delays (due partly to the Depression) resulted in Grace Cathedral's consecration being postponed until 1964. Described by its main architect, Lewis P. Hobart, as "a truly American cathedral," the cathedral is in fact neo-Gothic in style, partly modeled on Notre Dame in Paris.

Through the doors The most impressive exterior feature is a pair of gilded bronze doors from the Lorenzo Ghiberti cast that was used for the Gates of Paradise doors of the Baptistery in Florence. Inside, a 15th-century French altarpiece and an exquisite Flemish reredos can be seen in the Chapel of Grace, while the stained-glass windows depict biblical scenes and diverse achievers such as Albert Einstein and Henry Ford. The cathedral has, controversially, frequently hosted radical figures invited to speak from its pulpit.

Grace Cathedral took more than 50 years to build

CABLE CAR MUSEUM

The ring of the cable car bell provides a constant reminder that you are in San Francisco, probably the only city in the world where a relatively inefficient form of public transportation is adored by the entire population.

Inspired Legend has it that a horse, falling while trying to drag its load up a San Franciscan hill, inspired Andrew Smith Hallidie—a Scots-born manufacturer of wire rope who arrived in California in 1852—to invent the cable car. Wire rope had previously been used as a means of transporting materials in gold mines, but Hallidie was the first to develop the idea as a means of moving people. Besides improving transportation throughout the city, the cable car facilitated the settlement of Nob Hill. Damage caused by the 1906 earthquake and fire, and the subsequent rise of motorized transportation, soon rendered cable cars obsolete. Pressure from San Franciscans led the federal government to award National Historic Landmark status to cable cars in 1964, however, and a provision in the city's charter ensures the preservation of the three remaining lines.

Simple but effective The museum's intriguing memorabilia, including the first cable car, tell the story of the system's development. The clever engineering principle that keeps the cars running is also revealed: each one is pulled by an underground cable that never stops moving. The "gripman" on each car uses a lever to connect or disconnect the car to or from the cable through a slot in the road. The whirring sound, audible as you enter the museum, is the noise made by the steel cable as it is pulled over 14-foot-wide winding wheels, a process visible in the museum's lower level.

DID YOU KNOW?

- First cable car run: August 2, 1873
- First route: Clay Street
- Most cars in use: 600
- Most miles of track: 112
- Current number of cars in use: 38
- Current miles of track: 11
- Depth of cable beneath street: 18 inches
- Width of cable: 1¼ inches
- Average speed of cable car: 9½mph
- Annual cable car passengers: 10,500,000

INFORMATION

- K4
- 1201 Mason Street
- 415/474-1887
- Apr–Oct daily 10–6. Nov–Mar daily 10–5
- 1, 30, 45, 83; Powell–Mason or Powell–Hyde cable car
- Few; good on lower level
- Free
- Grace Cathedral (➤ 40), Chinatown (➤ 50), Nob Hill (➤ 50), Old St. Mary's Church (➤ 52), Tien Hou Temple (➤ 52), North Beach Museum (➤ 53), Bank of Canton (➤ 55), Huntington Park (➤ 56), Ina Coolbrith Park (➤ 56), Fairmont Hotel (➤ 57), Waverly Place (➤ 60)

ANSEL ADAMS CENTER

DID YOU KNOW?

Ansel Adams: 1902–1984
- Born in San Francisco
- First visit to Yosemite National Park: June, 1916
- First photo: Half Dome, Yosemite National Park, June, 1916
- First published book of photos: 1930
- Cofounder in 1967 of the Friends of Photography, who now administer the Center
- Previous occupation: pianist
- Photos donated by Adams to Ansel Adams Center: 125

INFORMATION

- L6
- 250 Fourth Street
- 415/495–7000
- Tue–Sun 11–5; first Thu of month 11–8
- 12, 15, 30, 45, 76
- Powell Street
- Excellent
- Moderate
- San Francisco Museum of Modern Art (➤ 44), SoMa (➤ 51), Cartoon Art Museum (➤ 53), Marriott Hotel (➤ 54), Pacific Telephone Building (➤ 55), Pacific Bell Museum (➤ 59)
- Free tours. Lectures, films, other events

Those who doubt the power of photography to provide social comment and to raise questions about the world are well advised to visit the Ansel Adams Center, an outstanding showplace for enquiring and creative picture-taking.

The exhibitions The Center's five galleries stage around 15 exhibitions each year and at any given time the combined displays offer an absorbing and sometimes provocative blend of historical and contemporary work. Photographers from the United States and overseas—household names and comparative unknowns—are all represented, variously using the camera's ability to read faces, exploit juxtapositions, and even make landscapes resonate with emotion. Past exhibitions have ranged from Eadweard Muybridge's extraordinary panoramas of 1880s San Francisco, to Wendy Ewald's work in urban and rural communities of Mexico giving local children the opportunity to photograph themselves, their environment, and their community.

Photographic friends The Center is named after the award-winning photographer whose evocative landscapes, particularly those of Yosemite Valley and other national parks, encouraged the preservation of some of the country's most celebrated areas of natural beauty and encouraged countless other photographers to aim their lenses at the features of nature. In 1967, together with Brett Weston (the photographer son of photographer Edward Weston) and art critic Beaumont Newhall, Adams founded the Friends of Photography, an organization whose workshops earned a reputation for encouraging exploration of the camera's creative potential. The Friends currently run the Center.

CHINESE HISTORICAL SOCIETY OF AMERICA

The Chinese have been present for longer, and in greater numbers, than any other non-Anglo ethnic group in San Francisco, greatly contributing to the city's multicultural character.

Early days The Chinese arrived in California in force during the Gold Rush, but met racial hostility and the foreigners tax (ostensibly due from all non-U.S. citizens in California, but in practice only levied against the Chinese). They were unjustly blamed for the economic depression that followed the gold boom and were eventually forced into "Chinatown" communities, the largest being in San Francisco. With further immigration outlawed and the Manchu Dynasty exercising strict control over Chinese people both at home and overseas, Chinatown became populated almost exclusively by males who wore traditional dress and tied their hair in braids. Denied the comforts of traditional family life, many Chinese men gambled, smoked opium, joined the secret Chinese-American societies known as Tongs, and visited prostitutes to alleviate the boredom —activities that added to the area's mystique.

Recent times Not until the founding of the Chinese Republic in 1911 were the Chinese able to adopt Western ideas and modes of dress. By the 1920s, the restaurants and stores of Chinatown were becoming tourist attractions and the Chinese, expanded in numbers through the easing of immigration restrictions, steadily became an accepted part of city life. This tiny museum does an excellent job in outlining the story of the Chinese in California, with many revealing texts alongside exhibits that range from gold-mining paraphernalia and religious objects to a 19th-century opium pipe.

DID YOU KNOW?

- Chinese in California in 1851: 25,000
- Chinese employed on transcontinental railroad in late 1860s: 10,000
- Proportion of factory jobs held by Chinese in San Francisco in 1872: 50%
- Chinese in San Francisco in 1875: 46,000
- Chinese in San Francisco in 1882: 26,000
- Number of Chinatown opium dens in 1885: 26
- Chinese in San Francisco in 1900: 11,000
- Chinese immigrants to San Francisco, 1910–1940: 175,000
- Estimated Chinese-Americans in San Francisco today: 90,000

INFORMATION

- L4
- 650 Commercial Street
- 415/391–1188
- Tue–Thu noon–2
- 1, 15, 41
- None
- Free
- Transamerica Pyramid (➤ 45), Chinatown (➤ 50), Old St. Mary's Church (➤ 52), Tien Hou Temple (➤ 52), North Beach Museum (➤ 53), Bank of Canton (➤ 55), Transamerica Redwood Park (➤ 56), Waverly Place (➤ 60)

21

SAN FRANCISCO MUSEUM OF MODERN ART

HIGHLIGHTS

- *Woman with the Hat,* Matisse
- *Head in Three-quarter View,* Picasso
- *The Coffee Pot,* Picasso
- *Guardians of the Secret,* Pollock
- *Violin and Candlestick,* Braque
- Paul Klee drawings
- Charles and Ray Eames office furniture
- *The Flower Carrier,* Rivera
- Clyfford Still gallery
- East European photography

INFORMATION

- L5
- 151 Third Street
- 415/357–4000
- Tue–Sun 11–6; Thu 11–9. Closed Mon
- Good café ($)
- 12, 15, 30, 45, 76
- Excellent
- Moderate; free first Tue of month
- Ansel Adams Center (► 42), SoMa (► 51), Cartoon Art Museum (► 53), Marriott Hotel (► 54), Pacific Telephone Building (► 55), Pacific Bell Museum (► 59)
- Free tours daily. Lectures, films, other events

One of the few things San Francisco used to lack was a world-class modern art museum, but this state of affairs ended in January 1995 with the opening of the excellent new San Francisco Museum of Modern Art.

Second floor The core of the museum's permanent collections is shown in the second-floor galleries, which highlight painting and sculpture from 1900 to 1970. Among significant contributions from Europeans are Pablo Picasso's *Head in Three-quarter View* and *The Coffee Pot,* and Georges Braque's *Violin and Candlestick.* Be sure not to miss the museum's prize possession: Matisse's *Woman with the Hat,* painted in 1905 and a work that made a crucial contribution to what became the century's first radical art movement, fauvism. A striking complement of abstract expressionist canvases includes Jackson Pollock's *Guardians of the Secret,* contributions from Willem de Kooning, and the last work by color-field painter Barnett Newman. Latin-American artists are also given prominent space; among the best represented are the intriguing Mexican modernists Diego Rivera and Frida Kahlo.

Other galleries With 17,000 exhibits spread across six floors and over 200,000 square feet, the museum has the space to devote several special galleries to California art. In this section the canvases of Richard Diebenkorn, especially the artist's long-running Ocean Park series, have particular impact and relevance to the region, as do the 28 works donated by California-based abstract expressionist Clyfford Still. The museum is also equipped to stage provocative exhibitions in the emerging fields of video, computer, and interactive art.

TRANSAMERICA PYRAMID

The Transamerica Pyramid is San Francisco's most distinctive building and arguably the most innovative modern contribution to the city's skyline. Stepping inside is hard to resist although doing so may prove to be somewhat anticlimactic.

Perfect profile San Franciscans were slow to appreciate the splendor of the 853-foot-high building's unique profile, rising above the Financial District's forest of even-sided high-rises with a slowly tapering spire flanked by windowless wings and with a decorative spire rising for 212 feet above the 48th floor. Yet the Transamerica Pyramid adds greatly to the city skyline and has steadily been accepted since 1972. The building is particularly appealing at night, when the hollow spire is lit from within and casts a distinctive glow above the city.

Inside looking out The building is a place of work for the 1,500 employees of the 50 firms (most of them financial) who rent its office space. The owners, the Transamerica Corporation, grew from various companies built around the Bank of Italy (later renamed the Bank of America), which was established in San Francisco in 1904. Although various works of art are arranged around the first floor, the interior of the building holds little of interest save for the Observation Level on the 27th floor, which offers views to North Beach and beyond.

DID YOU KNOW?

- Architect: William L. Pereira & Associates
- Smallest floor: 48th, 45 feet per side
- Largest floor: 5th, 145 feet per side
- Angle of slope: 5 degrees
- Depth of excavation: 52 feet
- Number of floors: 48

INFORMATION

- L4
- 600 Montgomery Street
- Average restaurant on ground floor ($$)
- Mon–Fri 8:30–4:30
- 15, 41
- Good
- Free
- Chinese Historical Society of America (➤ 43), Wells Fargo Museum (➤ 46), Chinatown (➤ 50), Old St. Mary's Church (➤ 52), Tien Hou Temple (➤ 52), Bank of America HQ (➤ 54), Bank of Canton (➤ 55), Transamerica Redwood Park (➤ 56), Waverly Place (➤ 60)

23

WELLS FARGO MUSEUM

INFORMATION

- L4/5
- 420 Montgomery Street
- 415/396–2619
- Mon–Fri 9–5
- 1, 12, 15, 42; California Street cable car
- Good
- Free
- Chinese Historical Society of America (➤ 43), Transamerica Pyramid (➤ 45), Chinatown (➤ 50), Old St. Mary's Church (➤ 52), Tien Hou Temple (➤ 52), Bank of America HQ (➤ 54), Bank of Canton (➤ 55), Transamerica Redwood Park (➤ 56), Waverly Place (➤ 60)

The company may have grown into one of the leading U.S. financial institutions, but for many the name of Wells Fargo is synonymous with the early days of the American West, and this collection ably demonstrates the historic links.

Going west Having established an express mail service in the East by the 1840s, Henry Wells and William G. Fargo began viewing the opportunities offered by Gold Rush-era California with relish, and they opened an office in San Francisco in 1852. Whether buying, selling, or transporting gold, transferring funds or delivering mail, the company earned a reputation for trustworthiness in an era dominated by rogues. By 1861, Wells Fargo & Co. was operating the western leg of the famed Pony Express (which ran for only 18 months) and, by the late 1860s, monopolized the movement of mail across the western United States. In 1905 the mail delivery and banking divisions of the company were separated, when the latter combined with the Nevada Bank—founded by the San Francisco-based silver barons of the Comstock Lode—setting Wells Fargo on the path to becoming a major player in the world of American high finance.

Looking back A few steps from the site of the company's 1852 office, the Wells Fargo Museum (inside the Wells Fargo Bank) entertainingly documents the rise of the company. Sitting inside an 1860s stagecoach provides one highlight, but there is much more to see amid the clutter of a re-created Gold Rush-era Wells Fargo office: gold-weighing scales, bulky mining tools, gold coins, and numerous aging letters that miraculously survived their trip across the rutted tracks of the old West.

24

OAKLAND MUSEUM OF CALIFORNIA

If you only make one crossing of San Francisco Bay, make it to Oakland where the Oakland Museum of Californian Art, Ecology, and History, leads the way in documenting the extraordinary nature, history and art of the Golden State.

Nature The remarkable plant and animal life found in the high mountains, low deserts, and other habitats of California are revealed by the 38,000-square-foot Hall of Ecology's elaborate dioramas. The adjoining Aquatic California Gallery does a similar job for underwater life, illustrating the goings-on in California's rivers, bays, and hot springs, and beneath the ocean.

History Every episode in California's past is remembered here, thoughtfully explored and copiously documented. The collections are enhanced by interactive computers offering detailed information on particular exhibits, recorded commentaries from experts, and oral histories. From outlining the conflicts between indigenous Californians and the colonizing Spaniards, the collections come up to date with the rise of Californian computer companies and the invention of the mountain bike.

Californian art An imaginative selection of exhibits on the top floor of the museum demonstrates how the art of California has developed from 19th-century depictions of its untamed, natural beauty, through to the self-confidence of later 20th-century Californian artists such as semi-abstract painter Richard Diebenkorn and ceramicist Peter Voulkos. The photography collection includes outstanding contributions from Dorothea Lange and Maynard Dixon, both of whom were based in San Francisco.

HIGHLIGHTS

- *Yosemite Valley,* Bierstadt
- *Migrant Mother,* Lange
- Re-created Nevada City assay office
- Re-created "beatnik" coffee house
- Ness's custom motorcycles
- *California Miner with Packhorse,* Raschen
- *San Francisco, July 1849,* Davis

INFORMATION

- Off map at N3
- 1000 Oak Street, Oakland
- 510/238–2200. Recorded information: 510/834–2413
- Wed–Sat 10–5; Sun 12–7. Closed Mon and Tue
- Good café ($)
- Lake Merritt
- Excellent
- Moderate
- Free tours. Films, lectures, and events

BERKELEY CAMPUS

HIGHLIGHTS

- Sproul Plaza
- Sather Tower (also called the Campanile—carillon recitals on Sunday afternoons)
- Hearst Mining Building
- Phoebe A. Hearst Museum of Anthropology
- University Art Museum
- Sather Gate
- Lawrence Hall of Science
- Morrison Library
- Bancroft Library

INFORMATION

- ✚ Off map at N3
- ✉ Main Gate, Bancroft Way
- ☎ 510/642–INFO. Tour information: 510/549–7040
- ◉ Daylight hours recommended
- 🍴 None, but many good options close by
- Ⓟ Berkeley
- ♿ Good
- 💲 Free
- ❓ Free tours twice daily Mon, Wed and Fri

Children play on the DNA model on Berkeley campus

A haven of 1960s student dissent, the Berkeley campus might be less radical than it once was, but its buildings and museums and the picture it provides of contemporary Californian student life easily justify a trip.

Past The first college at Berkeley opened in the 1850s, but a lack of funds allowed the facility to be purchased in 1873 by the state government as the first of what are now six campuses of the University of California. Much of the university's early finance came as donations from Phoebe Apperson Hearst, wife of a wealthy mining baron and mother of the even more wealthy publishing tycoon, William Randolph Hearst. In the 1940s, Robert Oppenheimer was Berkeley's professor of physics before moving to Los Alamos to work on the first atomic bomb. In 1964, the seeds of what evolved into country-wide student rebellions were sown by the sit-ins and rallies of Berkeley's Free Speech Movement.

Present Nowadays, Berkeley's 30,000 students are more concerned with acquiring a good degree than immersing themselves in radical politics, though there is no shortage of causes and campaigns being promoted along Sproul Plaza, in the heart of the campus, on any weekday lunchtime. Elsewhere around the 100-acre campus is a selection of museums, libraries, and architecturally distinguished buildings such as John Galen Howard's *beaux-arts*-style Hearst Mining Building. Galen was also responsible for the elegant Sather Gate, which marks the main entrance to the campus opposite Telegraph Avenue.

SAN FRANCISCO's
best

NEIGHBORHOODS

Fisherman's Wharf

Directly north of North Beach is Fisherman's Wharf, the only section of San Francisco pitched squarely at visitors. Former factories and fishing piers have been carefully and imaginatively converted to complexes of stores, restaurants, and tourist attractions. Despite the obvious commercial trappings, Fisherman's Wharf draws 12 million visitors each year and is, for most, an enjoyable experience.

A street in Chinatown

CHINATOWN

The compact streets and alleyways of Chinatown's 24 history-laden blocks are home to one of the largest Asian communities outside Asia. Several 100-year-old temples, fortune-cookie factories, and numerous exotic stores are crammed into one of the city's most energetic and ethnically distinct neighborhoods. The area also holds some of the city's best-value restaurants, inexpensive and excellent almost without fail.

✚ K/L4/5 ▣ 1, 15, 30, 45, 83; California Street cable car

HAIGHT-ASHBURY

Holding hundreds of elegant Victorian homes that survived the 1906 earthquake and fire, and becoming world-famous as the heart of hippiedom in 1967, Haight-Ashbury has long been the most tolerant section of a tolerant city. It holds exceptional used-book stores and vintage clothing outlets, and remains a lively center for alternative arts, culture, and lifestyles.

✚ F–H6–8 ▣ 6, 7, 24, 33, 43, 66, 71

JAPANTOWN

A concentration of Japanese temples, stores, and restaurants, and Japanese-style residential architecture, make this the spiritual home of San Francisco's Japanese-American population, even though comparatively few Japanese-Americans actually live here.

✚ H5 ▣ 2, 3, 4, 22, 38

MISSION DISTRICT

With Latin-American bakeries and restaurants, and some of its streets decorated by stunning murals (➤ 59), the Mission District holds the bulk of the city's Hispanic population. The neighborhood's Mexican-American population, established here in the 1940s, was joined from the 1970s by arrivals from Central America's war-torn countries.

✚ J/K7–9 ▣ 12, 14, 26, 33, 49, 67 ▣ 16th Street Mission, 24th Street Mission

NOB HILL

A quartet of extremely wealthy Californians (the "Big Four," ➤ 12) built the first million-dollar mansions on Nob Hill from the 1870s. The 1906 earthquake and fire destroyed all but one of the district's opulent homes, but Nob Hill's place as a rich person's stamping ground is still evident. The area holds exclusive hotels and a very well-dressed congregation shows up for Sunday services at the neighborhood's Grace Cathedral (➤ 40).

✚ K5 ▣ 1, 27; California Street cable car

Victorian houses near
Russian Hill

NORTH BEACH

North Beach's wealth of cafés—serving top-quality coffee and a formidable array of cakes and pastries—and bookstores recall its links with the Beat Generation of the 1950s. Meanwhile, the abundant Italian-owned restaurants and stores are reminders of the Italians who settled in the district in force from the late 19th century.

✚ K4 🚍 15, 30, 39, 41, 45, 83

PACIFIC HEIGHTS

Pacific Heights draws the wealthiest strata of San Franciscan society to its stately Victorian homes—some of them designed by architects who were attracted to California by the mid-19th-century Gold Rush—and high-rise luxury apartment buildings boasting wonderful views to Alcatraz and beyond.

✚ G–J4/5 🚍 1, 3, 22, 24, 41, 42, 45, 47, 49

RUSSIAN HILL

A noted bohemian enclave in the late 19th century, Russian Hill is still a home of writers and artists, though only those with established reputations—and commensurate incomes—can afford to live among the successful doctors and lawyers who inhabit this quiet and cozy neighborhood today.

✚ J/K3/4 🚍 41, 45; Powell–Hyde cable car

SOMA

Many of the former warehouses and factories of SoMa, an abbreviation of "South of Market Street," have been transformed into nightclubs, restaurants, and the offices of media companies. The biggest boost has been the development of the 12-block Yerba Buena Gardens cultural complex.

✚ J–M5–7 🚍 10, 12, 14, 15, 20, 26, 27, 30, 45, 50, 60, 70, 76, 80

The Castro

The rainbow flags of gay solidarity are a common sight above the streets of the Castro, west of the Mission District, settled in large numbers by gay men (and by lesser numbers of lesbians) from the 1970s. As gays campaigned for and won a voice in city politics, the Castro evolved into the world's largest and most famous gay neighborhood.

PLACES OF WORSHIP

Old St. Mary's Church

St. John's African Orthodox Church

St. John's African Orthodox Church, also known as "the Church of John Coltrane," was founded in 1971 by a jazz fan who underwent a religious experience when hearing saxophonist John Coltrane play live in the 1960s. The fan is now a sax-playing bishop who leads a congregation that is encouraged to bring instruments and to play them during the services.

> **See Top 25 Sights for**
> **GRACE CATHEDRAL ➤ 40**
> **MISSION DOLORES ➤ 34**
> **ST. MARY'S CATHEDRAL ➤ 36**

CHURCH OF SAINTS PETER AND PAUL
Long the major place of worship for North Beach's Italian community, this imposing Romanesque edifice was founded in 1922. The twin spires rise above Washington Square and are evocatively illuminated at night.

➕ K4 ✉ 666 Filbert Street ☎ 415/421–0809 🕐 Usually 7:30AM–8PM 🚌 15, 30, 39, 41, 45 💲 Free

OLD ST. MARY'S CHURCH
The West Coast's first Catholic cathedral and a forerunner of today's ultramodern St. Mary's Cathedral (➤ 36), Old St. Mary's was completed in 1854.

➕ K5 ✉ 660 California Street ☎ 415/288–3800 🕐 Mon–Fri, Sun 7–3:30; Sat 11–6 🚌 1, 15; California Street cable car 💲 Free

ST. JOHN'S AFRICAN ORTHODOX CHURCH
Almost certainly the most curious church in San Francisco (see panel for details).

➕ H7 ✉ 351 Divisadero Street ☎ 415/621–4054 🕐 Service: Sun from 10AM; Wed 6PM 🚌 24

SWEDENBORGIAN CHURCH
In keeping with Swedenborgian beliefs, this diminutive church resembles a finely crafted log cabin. Completed in 1895, the church was the work of several leading figures of the California Arts and Crafts movement.

➕ G5 ✉ 2107 Lyon Street ☎ 415/346–6466 🕐 Mon–Fri 9–5 🚌 3, 43 💲 Free

TEMPLE EMANU-EL
This immense Byzantine-style structure, able to seat 2,000 people, looms above the surrounding residential architecture. Finished in 1926 at a cost of $3 million, the temple was raised to serve the longest-established Jewish congregation in California.

➕ F5 ✉ Lake Street and Arguello Boulevard ☎ 415/751–2535 🕐 Guided tours only: Mon–Fri 1–3 🚌 1, 4, 33 💲 Free

TIEN HOU TEMPLE
Dating from 1852, this is the oldest and most atmospheric of Chinatown's incense-charged temples. Offerings of fruit, commonly oranges or tangerines, are placed before the altar by believers.

➕ K4 ✉ Fourth floor, 125 Waverly Place 🕐 Erratic, but usually Mon–Sat 10:30–4 🚌 1, 15, 30, 45, 83 💲 Donation, inexpensive

MUSEUMS

CARTOON ART MUSEUM

Be they from comics, T.V., or the movies or culled from the deepest recesses of history—cartoons are accorded the seriousness of art in the changing exhibitions staged here, these seldom failing to be thought-provoking and entertaining.

➕ L6 ✉ 814 Mission Street ☎ 415/227-8666 🕓 Wed–Fri 11–5; Sat 10–5; Sun 1–5 🚍 15, 30, 45 💰 Moderate

NATIONAL MARITIME MUSEUM

A fine collection of figureheads, model ships, and other nautical memorabilia recalls San Francisco's seafaring and shipbuilding past. The building itself resembles an ocean liner and provides a fine example of the 1930s art deco Streamline Moderne style.

➕ J3 ✉ Aquatic Park, foot of Polk Street ☎ 415/556-3002 🕓 Daily 10AM–5PM 🚍 19, 32; Powell–Hyde cable car 💰 Free

NORTH BEACH MUSEUM

Temporary exhibitions of photographs and paraphernalia document various episodes in the eventful past of this distinctive neighborhood.

➕ K4 ✉ Mezzanine level, 1435 Stockton Street ☎ 415/391-6210 🕓 Mon–Thu 9–4; Fri 9–6 🚍 30, 45 💰 Free

TATTOO ART MUSEUM

The posters, prints, and photographs lining the walls of this working tattoo parlor reveal some of the more extreme examples of the tattooist's art. Meanwhile, a selection of gruesome tattooists' tools from times past suggest this form of body decoration has never been a popular option for the faint-hearted.

➕ K4 ✉ 841 Columbus Avenue ☎ 415/775-4991 🕓 Usually noon–9 or 10PM 🚍 15, 30 💰 Free

A submarine tour

After touring the National Maritime Museum, continue the nautical theme by exploring the claustrophobic innards of USS *Pampanito*, moored a few minutes' walk away at Pier 45. Launched in 1943, the submarine saw action in the Pacific and sank 27,000 tons of enemy shipping. The cramped crews' and officers' quarters, the engine rooms, and the torpedo room are included on a self-guided tour.

Moebius's "The Major," in the Cartoon Art Museum

MODERN BUILDINGS

See Top 25 Sights for
ST. MARY'S CATHEDRAL ➤ 36
SAN FRANCISCO MUSEUM OF
MODERN ART ➤ 44
TRANSAMERICA PYRAMID ➤ 45

Art and architecture

Besides holding an excellent art collection, the San Francisco Museum of Modern Art (➤ 44) is also a distinguished architectural addition to the city. Opened in 1995, the $60-million museum was designed by Swiss architect Mario Botta, who gave it a stepped-back brick and stone façade. A truncated cylinder rising through the center allows light to flood the interior's full-height atrium.

The ultramodern architecture of the Rincon Center is complemented by this decorative stylus

BANK OF AMERICA HQ

No longer owned by the bank whose name it bears but still a supreme example of inspired 1960s high-rise office architecture. The 52-story building's dark red exterior, dominating the area by day, seems to become almost transparent at sunset.

➕ L5 ✉ 555 California Street 🚇 15, 42; California Street cable car

101 CALIFORNIA STREET

This Philip Johnson/John Burgee office tower is a soaring glass-sided silo that masquerades as a greenhouse at ground level.

➕ L5 ✉ 101 California Street 🚇 California Street cable car

CIRCLE GALLERY

During the late 1940s, architect Frank Lloyd Wright undertook a complete remodeling of this 1911 building and the design provided a foretaste of his acclaimed Guggenheim Museum in New York. The exterior brickwork is imbued with Mayan motifs; go inside to find the distinctive spiral ramp.

➕ K5 ✉ 140 Maiden Lane 🚇 2, 3, 4, 30, 45

GHIRARDELLI SQUARE

One of Fisherman's Wharf's successful conversions, the red-brick shell of the chocolate factory that opened here in 1893 now holds a strollable complex of stores and restaurants.

➕ J3 ✉ 900 North Point Street 🚇 19, 42; Powell–Hyde cable car

MARRIOTT HOTEL

A voluminous 40-story structure, the largest building in the city, the hotel sharply divided opinion when it opened in 1989. Newspaper columnist Herb Caen derisively dubbed it the "jukebox Marriott."

➕ L5 ✉ 777 Market Street 🚇 5, 6, 7, 8, 9, 21, 31, 38

RINCON CENTER

An office and shopping complex grafted with great style onto the rear of a 1930s art deco post office. The latter retains a vibrant 1939 mural depicting scenes from California's history.

➕ L/M5 ✉ Mission Street, between Spear and Steuart Streets 🚇 14

HISTORIC BUILDINGS

BANK OF CANTON
A three-tiered, pagoda-style structure erected in 1909 as the Chinatown telephone exchange; it was converted into a bank in the 1950s.
✚ K4 ✉ 743 Washington Street 🚌 1, 15, 30, 45

FERRY BUILDING
Completed in 1903, the 235-foot-high Ferry Building was for many years the city's tallest structure. Surviving the 1906 earthquake and fire—and a plan to demolish it for safety reasons during the disaster—the slender tower became a symbol of San Francisco's ability to survive natural catastrophe.
✚ M4 ✉ Foot of Market Street 🚌 5, 6, 7, 8, 9, 21, 31

HASS LILIENTHAL HOUSE
This elaborate 1886 example of the vertically exaggerated "stick" style of architecture is also the only San Franciscan Victorian building to retain period-furnished rooms.
✚ J4 ✉ 2007 Franklin Street 🕐 Guided tours Wed 12–3:15; Sun 11–4:30 🚌 83 👐 Moderate

LEVI STRAUSS FACTORY
Built by Levi Strauss after the 1906 earthquake and still producing the world-famous jeans.
✚ J7 ✉ 250 Valencia Street ☎ 415/565–9153 🕐 Guided tours on selected dates by appointment 🚌 26

OCTAGON HOUSE
One of five eight-sided houses built in San Francisco, their shape considered lucky by the owners, the Octagon House dates from 1861. The restoration was organized by the Colonial Dames of America whose exhibitions of Colonial- and Federal-period arts and crafts now fill the interior.
✚ H4 ✉ 2645 Gough Street 🚌 41, 45

PACIFIC TELEPHONE BUILDING
A stylish skyscraper of the 1920s, its design heavily influenced by the work of Eliel Saarinen.
✚ L5 ✉ 140 New Montgomery Street 🚌 5, 6, 7, 8, 9, 15, 21, 30, 31, 38, 45, 71

VEDANTA TEMPLE
An extraordinary conglomeration of turquoise-colored towers, turrets, and domes, built in 1905 for an esoteric Eastern religious sect.
✚ H4 ✉ 2963 Webster Street 🚌 22, 41, 45

Octagon House

Levi's jeans

German-born entrepreneur Levi Strauss arrived in San Francisco in 1853 and began manufacture of what he called a "waist-high overall" for use by workers in the Californian gold mines. Hard-wearing, with tough seams, copper rivets, and numerous pockets, the Strauss garments evolved into "jeans", their popularity spreading across the American West and around the world.

GREEN SPACES

See Top 25 Sights for
**GOLDEN GATE NATIONAL
RECREATION AREA ➤ 24
GOLDEN GATE PARK ➤ 25**

Angel Island State Park

For a day in the wilds, make the short ferry crossing from Fisherman's Wharf to the mile-square Angel Island. The largest piece of land in San Francisco Bay, the island is a state park with foot trails and bike paths navigating its thickly forested heart. Also explorable are the remains of a military prison and of an immigration processing center.

Washington Square, North Beach

HUNTINGTON PARK

Facing Grace Cathedral (➤ 40), Huntington Park occupies the plot of an 1872 mansion and is named after one of the "Big Four" railroad barons (➤ 12). ✚ K5 ✉ Bordered by California, Sacramento, Taylor, and Cushman Streets 🚋 1; California Street cable car

INA COOLBRITH PARK

A tiny but abundantly vegetated park accessed by steps and named for the woman who, in 1919, became California's first poet laureate. Coolbrith's literary get-togethers, held at her Russian Hill home, were legendary. ✚ K4 ✉ Bordered by Taylor and Vallejo Streets 🚋 Powell–Mason cable car

LAFAYETTE PARK

The highest point in Pacific Heights and overlooked by the splendid Spreckels Mansion, completed in 1912 as the home of sugar-baron Adolph Spreckels and his wife. ✚ H/J5 ✉ Bordered by Gough, Laguna, Sacramento, and Washington Streets 🚋 1, 12

MARINA GREEN

Kite-flying, jogging, and the walking of well-bred dogs are among the popular pursuits in this bay-side green strip, overlooked by pastel-colored stucco-fronted houses and serving an affluent neighborhood. ✚ G/H3 ✉ Beside Marina Boulevard 🚋 22

TRANSAMERICA REDWOOD PARK

Located behind the Transamerica Pyramid (➤ 45) and a welcome break from the hubbub of the Financial District, this slender park holds young redwood trees and stages free lunchtime concerts on weekdays. ✚ L4 ✉ Bordered by Washington and Clay Streets 🚋 15, 41

WASHINGTON SQUARE

Packed each morning with Chinese going through their *t'ai chi* routines, this North Beach park is also the scene for enjoyable art shows each weekend. ✚ K4 ✉ Bordered by Columbus Avenue, and Filbert, Union, and Stockton Streets 🚋 15, 30, 39, 41, 45

VIEWS

See Top 25 Sights for
**PALACE OF THE LEGION OF
HONOR ► 26
TRANSAMERICA PYRAMID ► 45**

ALAMO SQUARE
Perhaps the most-photographed view in San Francisco finds the six Victorian homes, or "painted ladies," on the east side of Alamo Square contrasting with the modern towers of the Financial District visible in the background.
✚ H6 ⊠ Bordered by Hayes, Fulton, Scott, and Steiner Streets 🚌 21

COIT TOWER
Whether from the top of the tower or from its base, the outlook across San Francisco Bay and a huge swath of the city is a memorable one.
✚ K3 ⊠ Summit of Telegraph Hill Boulevard 🚌 39

FAIRMONT HOTEL CROWN ROOM ELEVATOR
The glass-sided elevator that rises nonstop from ground level to the 22nd-floor Crown Room restaurant brings vertiginous views of the Financial District as it recedes far below.
✚ K5 ⊠ 950 Mason Street 🚌 1; California Street cable car

SUTRO HEIGHTS PARK
From the former grounds of the home of legendary 19th-century San Francisco benefactor Adolph Sutro are fabulous views of the city's Pacific coast and the western end of Golden Gate Park. Remnants of the house and its statuary are scattered about the park's footpaths.
✚ A6 ⊠ Bordered by Point Lobos Avenue, Great Highway, and 48th Street 🚌 18, 38

TWIN PEAKS
One of the best overall views of San Francisco comes, not surprisingly, from one of its highest points, the 913-foot summit of the two hills known as Twin Peaks; even on foot, the exhausting ascent is worthwhile.
✚ G9 ⊠ Summit of Twin Peaks Boulevard 🚌 37

*The view from
Twin Peaks*

Coit Tower's murals
While the external view is one reason for visiting Coit Tower, another is the excellent murals lining its interior walls. Painted as part of a Depression era project to give work to artists, the left-wing political content of the murals—by several artists and showing Californian scenes—caused great controversy during the early 1930s and delayed the tower's official opening.

ATTRACTIONS FOR CHILDREN

See Top 25 Sights for
CABLE CAR MUSEUM ➤ 41
CALIFORNIA ACADEMY OF SCIENCES ➤ 30
EXPLORATORIUM ➤ 32
HYDE STREET PIER HISTORICAL SHIPS ➤ 39
WELLS FARGO MUSEUM ➤ 46

BEACHES
China and Baker beaches (part of Golden Gate National Recreation Area, ➤ 24) make appealing locations for enjoying a picnic and a frolic in the sand. The sea lions of Seal Rocks might provide sufficient incentive for embarking on the scenically dramatic coastal trail.

CABLE CAR RIDE
Any cable car is an enjoyable adventure for most children, but to avoid the lines at the main embarkation points take the California Street line, which includes a dramatic climb to (and descent from) Nob Hill.
✉ Operate on three routes (➤ 90–91) ☎ General public transport information: 415/673–MUNI ⏰ Hours of operation: 6AM–1AM 💲 Inexpensive

Few can resist a ride on a cable car

JOSEPHINE S. RANDALL JUNIOR MUSEUM
A zoo with animals to pet and a nature walk are the main attractions, but there are also science exhibits—such as a mineral collection and a seismograph—to entertain and inform young minds.
➕ H8 ✉ 199 Museum Way ☎ 415/554–9600 ⏰ Tue–Sun 10–5 🚌 37 💲 Free

RIPLEY'S BELIEVE IT OR NOT!
An 8-foot-long cable car made from 275,000 matchsticks, a display about the man who could whistle while holding three golf balls in his mouth, and a room devoted to a simulated Californian earthquake are among the mass of strangely compelling delights that children are likely to relish.
➕ K3 ✉ 175 Jefferson Street ☎ 415/771–6188 ⏰ Sun–Thu 10–10; Fri–Sat 10–midnight 🚌 15, 30, 32, 39, 42; Powell–Mason cable car 💲 Moderate

SAN FRANCISCO ZOOLOGICAL GARDENS
Awkwardly located on the fringes of the city, this zoo nevertheless holds the usual complement of creatures, plus a state-of-the-art primate center and a Children's Zoo where furry creatures aplenty can be stroked.
➕ Off map at B10 ✉ Sloat Boulevard and 45th Avenue ☎ 415/753–7080. Recorded information: 415/753–7083 ⏰ Daily 10–5 🚌 18, 23; L 💲 Moderate; free first Wed of each month

Pier 39's sea lions
Introducing young minds to the wonders of natural California can easily be accomplished at Fisherman's Wharf's Pier 39. Attracted by an abundant supply of herring, some 600 California sea lions have made their homes beside the pier and can be observed from a marked viewing area. A naturalist arrives to talk about the creatures most weekend afternoons (for details: ☎ 415/289–7325).

FREE ATTRACTIONS

Hotel art

Public areas in San Franciscan hotels can prove rewarding for art and photography enthusiasts: The Palace (➤ 84) has an excellent Maxfield Parrish mural; Gustav Klimt prints line the Redwood Room at The Clift (➤ 81); and the Compass Rose Room at the Westin St. Francis (➤ 84) holds photographs by Ansel Adams.

CHINESE CULTURAL CENTER
On the third floor of the towering Holiday Inn—which looms above Portsmouth Square and its legions of elderly Chinese men indulging in games of chance—are rotating exhibitions that explore diverse aspects of Chinese culture and artistic traditions.
➕ L4 ✉ Holiday Inn, 750 Kearny Street ☎ 415/986–1822
🕐 Tue–Sat 10–4 🚌 15

DIEGO RIVERA GALLERY
An immense mural by the Mexican master, Diego Rivera, sits at one end of this gallery of the highly respected San Francisco Institute of Art, while student works line the other three walls.
➕ J3 ✉ 800 Chestnut Street ☎ 415/771–7020 🕐 Mon–Fri 9–5 🚌 15, 30, 41; Powell–Hyde cable car

FORT POINT NATIONAL HISTORIC SITE
Completed in 1861, Fort Point was intended to deter enemy incursions into San Francisco Bay but never a shot was fired in anger. Period-attired guides describe the fort's past, while temporary indoor exhibitions explore diverse aspects of U.S. military history.
➕ D3 ✉ Beneath Golden Gate Bridge ☎ 415/556–1693
🕐 Wed–Sun 10–5 🚌 28, 29, 76

MISSION DISTRICT MURALS
Some of the best of the Mission District's many murals, reflecting Latin-American muralist traditions, line this alley and focus on a theme of peace in Central America. Visit during daylight hours.
➕ K9 ✉ Balmy Alley, between 24th and 25th Streets
☎ 415/285–2287 (Precita Eyes Mural Center) 🚌 12, 27, 67

PACIFIC BELL MUSEUM
The Pacific Bell is located on the ground floor of the eye-catching Pacific Telephone Building (➤ 55). The museum documents communications past, present, and future, with displays on everything from ancient switchboards to satellite technology.
➕ L5 ✉ 140 New Montgomery Street ☎ 415/542–0182
🕐 Mon–Fri 10–3 🚌 5, 6, 7, 8, 9, 15, 21, 30, 31, 38, 45, 71

Afro-American mural in the Mission District

59

INTRIGUING STREETS

Filbert Steps

Steep gradients are a San Franciscan specialty and often cause streets to become flights of steps. One such is the Filbert Steps, running between Telegraph Hill (from Coit Tower) and Levi's Plaza. Curiously, the gardens that line Filbert Steps are the result of the horticultural enterprise of a one-time Hollywood stunt lady, who moved here on her retirement in 1949.

GREEN STREET
Among the numerous architecturally distinguished survivors of the 1906 earthquake and fire along this single block are the Feusier Octagon House, number 1067, one of the city's two remaining eight-sided homes (▶ 55).
🚋 J/K4 ✉ Between Jones and Leavenworth Streets 🚌 41, 45; Powell–Hyde cable car

LOMBARD STREET
Traffic zigzags down Lombard Street, "the crookedest street in San Francisco," at 5mph, moving around colorful gardens put in place during the 1920s.
🚋 J4 ✉ Between Hyde and Leavenworth Streets 🚌 15, 19, 30

MACONDRAY LANE
With leafy trees shading its cottages, most of which were raised in the construction boom that followed the 1906 earthquake, pedestrianized Macondray Lane is the epitome of quaint and cozy Russian Hill.
🚋 J/K4 ✉ Between Taylor and Leavenworth Streets 🚌 41, 45; Powell–Hyde cable car

MAIDEN LANE
Notorious for its brothels in the 1800s, Maiden Lane is now lined by upscale shops and bordered by fancy wooden gates.
🚋 K/L5 ✉ Between Stockton and Kearny Streets 🚌 2, 3, 4, 30, 45

UNION STREET
The affluent and fashionable residents of Pacific Heights shop, eat, and socialize along these few chic blocks.
🚋 H/J4 ✉ Between Franklin and Steiner Streets 🚌 22, 41, 45

VALENCIA STREET
A Mission District thoroughfare known for its smattering of feminist- and women's-interest shops and cafés amid anonymous warehouses and car-repair workshops.
🚋 J8/9 ✉ Between 16th and 24th Streets 🚌 26

WAVERLY PLACE
A Chinatown side street holding three temples, numerous Chinese family association buildings, and the decorations that earn it the name "street of painted balconies."
🚋 K4/5 ✉ Between Sacramento and Washington Streets 🚌 1, 15, 30, 45, 83

SAN FRANCISCO
where to...

EXPENSIVE RESTAURANTS

Prices

Average meal per head
excluding drink:

$ = up to $15

$$ = up to $30

$$$ = over $30

Except for the luxury restaurants
on this page, where dinner will
easily cost upwards of $80
excluding wine for two people
(lunch will be less; typically
around $40), dining in San
Francisco is a cost-effective
experience. Anticipate spending
$6–$8 per person for breakfast,
around $10 for lunch, and
$15–$20 for dinner excluding
drinks. Wherever you dine, a tip
of at least 15 percent of the
total is expected; reward
extremely good service with a
tip of 20 percent or more.

Opening times

Peak hours for lunch are
11:30–2, and for dinner
5:30–9, but many restaurants
open earlier and/or close later
than these times.

ACT IV
Californian cuisine
with a Mediterranean
slant; a favorite haunt of
visiting opera and
theater stars.
➕ J6 ✉ Inn at the Opera
Hotel, 333 Fulton Street
☎ 415/553–8100
🕐 No lunch on weekends
🚌 5, 21

AQUA
Carefully prepared and
presented seafood draws
a style-conscious crowd
to this modernistic
eaterie.
➕ L4 ✉ 252 California Street
☎ 415/956–9662 🚌 1, 41;
California Street cable car

CAFÉ MAJESTIC
Inventive Californian
dishes with a European
twist; the Edwardian
dining room is regularly
heralded as San
Francisco's most
romantic dining spot.
➕ J5 ✉ 1500 Sutter Street
☎ 415/776–6400 🕐 No
lunch weekends or Mon 🚌 2, 4

CAMPTON PLACE
The ever-changing
menu reflects the fact
that only the freshest
local produce is used to
create dishes especially
valued for their natural
flavors.
➕ K5 ✉ Campton Place Hotel,
340 Stockton Street
☎ 415/955–5555 🚌 30, 45

FLEUR DE LYS
More formal than
many—jacket and tie
required—and serving
San Francisco's best
French food.
➕ K5 ✉ 777 Sutter Street
☎ 415/673–7779 🕐 Dinner
only 🚌 2, 3, 4, 7

MASA'S
A very fine Californian-
French restaurant
renowned for its quality.
Usually booked weeks
in advance, although
cancellations can make
tables available at
short notice.
➕ K5 ✉ Vintage Court Hotel,
648 Bush Street ☎ 415/989–
7154 🕐 Dinner only; closed
Sun, Mon 🚌 2, 3, 4, 30, 76

POSTRIO
Run by celebrity chef
Wolfgang Puck and the
epitome of California-
style gourmet dining,
utilizing fresh local
produce.
➕ K5 ✉ 545 Post Street
☎ 415/776–7825
🚌 2, 3, 4, 76

SILKS
A blend of contemporary
American cuisine and
Asian subtlety in an
elegant setting.
➕ L5 ✉ Mandarin Oriental
Hotel, 222 Sansome Street
☎ 415/986–2020 🚌 42

STARS
Hot spot for socialites
and gossip columnists;
varied fare but usually
strongest on seafood.
➕ J6 ✉ 150 Redwood Street
☎ 415/861–7827
🕐 No lunch on weekends
🚌 5, 42, 47, 49

TOMMY TOY'S
French and Chinese
influences combine in
an imaginative menu;
the setting is an opulent
one and the service is
famously attentive.
➕ L4 ✉ 655 Montgomery
Street ☎ 415/397–4888
🕐 No lunch on weekends
🚌 15, 41

INDIAN & VEGETARIAN RESTAURANTS

INDIAN

APPAM, CUISINE OF OLD INDIA ($$)
Uses the traditional Dum Pakht method of cooking in a sealed pot.
+ K7 ✉ 1259 Folsom Street
☎ 415/626–2798 🚌 12, 76

GAYLORD INDIA RESTAURANT ($$)
With striking views across the Golden Gate, Gaylord specializes in northern Indian fare.
+ J3 ✉ Ghirardelli Square, 900 North Point Street
☎ 415/771–8822 🚌 19, 42

INDIA CLAY OVEN ($$)
Tempting Indian staples plus many more innovative dishes; or try the seven-course Chef's Thali, a house specialty offered for dinner.
+ D6 ✉ 2345 Clement Street ☎ 415/751–0505
🚌 2

MAHARANI ($–$$)
Friendly Indian eatery with good prices and a menu that includes many vegetarian dishes.
+ J5 ✉ 1122 Post Street
☎ 415/775–1988 🚌 42

NORTH INDIA ($$)
The setting adds to the atmosphere and the hotter dishes are more spicy than those at most Indian restaurants.
+ H4 ✉ 3131 Webster Street ☎ 415/931–1556
🚌 22, 41, 46

STAR OF INDIA ($)
Many mouthwatering vegetarian selections help to make this one of San Francisco's more appealing Indian eateries; the weekday lunch buffet is exceptional value.
+ F6 ✉ 3721 Geary Boulevard ☎ 415/668–4466
🚌 38

TANDOORI MAHAL ($$)
An elegantly decorated dining room and a long list of classily prepared dishes; great-value lunchtime buffet.
+ K4 ✉ 941 Kearny Street
☎ 415/951–0505 🚌 15

VEGETARIAN

ANANDA FUARA ($)
A serene atmosphere prevails at this restaurant, run by an (unobtrusive) religious sect; "meatloaf" served with gravy and potatoes is one popular option.
+ J6 ✉ 1298 Market Street
☎ 415/621–1994 🚌 6, 7, 66, 71 🚇 Van Ness

GREENS ($$$)
Gourmet-pleasing dishes are created here using the produce of an organic farm run at a Zen Buddhist retreat on the north side of San Francisco Bay. The bay views are as stunning as the food; reservations are essential.
+ H3 ✉ Building A, Fort Mason Culture Center
☎ 415/771–7955
🚌 22, 28, 30, 47, 49

VEGI FOOD ($)
Intriguing and inviting vegetarian dishes are on offer here, mostly based on Chinese cuisine.
+ D6 ✉ 1820 Clement Street ☎ 415/387–8111
🚌 2

Sourdough bread

The slightly bitter and chewy sourdough bread served in many San Franciscan restaurants first appeared here during the Gold Rush (and was first baked commercially by a French San Franciscan settler called Isadore Boudin). Yeast and baking powder were scarce and settlers made bread using a sour starter, a fermented mixture of flour and water that enabled the dough to rise. San Franciscan folklore holds that the quality of a sourdough loaf is dependent upon the local fog.

BUDGET RESTAURANTS

ART INSTITUTE CAFÉ
Simple pasta dishes and assorted snacks can be consumed while enjoying the splendid view across the local rooftops to San Francisco Bay; part of San Francisco Art Institute.

J3 · 800 Chestnut Street · 415/749–4567 · Lunch · 15, 30, 41; Powell–Hyde cable car

DOTTIE'S TRUE BLUE CAFÉ
Small, friendly diner with great start-the-day omelets and a variety of healthy lunches.

K5 · 522 Jones Street · 415/885–2767 · Breakfast and lunch · 27

EAGLE CAFÉ
Serving well-filled omelets and substantial sandwiches since the 1920s and providing an authentic slice of local life in a touristy area; order at the counter and wait for your number to be called.

K3 · Pier 39 · 415/433–3689 · Breakfast and lunch · 32

EL TORO TAQUERIA
Burritos in many varieties and other low-cost, well-prepared Mexican favorites are found in this busy eatery in the Hispanic Mission District.

J8 · 598 Valencia Street · 415/431–3351 · 26

HAMBURGER MARY'S ORGANIC GRILL
Garishly decorated and often patronized by a nightclubbing clientele, Mary's offers specialist burgers as well as a tempting selection of soups, sandwiches, and salads.

K7 · 1582 Folsom Street · 415/626–5767 · 12

MAX'S OPERA CAFÉ
While the food is affordable and filling New York-style deli fare such as sandwiches and salads, the real attraction is the opera-singing staff, who strut their stuff each evening.

J6 · 601 Van Ness Avenue · 415/771–7300 · 5, 42, 47, 49

MIFUNE
Fast food Japanese style, served to fast-moving customers; includes simple but excellent noodle dishes and much more to delight.

H5 · 1737 Post Street · 415/922–0337 · 38

NORTH BEACH PIZZA
The thick, chewy pizzas served with a host of toppings are famous throughout the city and often result in a line forming outside in the evenings; a newer branch is down the hill at 1310 Grant Avenue.

K4 · 1499 Grant Avenue · 415/433–2444 · Lunch and dinner · 15, 30, 41, 45

WORLD WRAPPS
Burritos offered with a host of exotic fillings; Thai chicken is just one of many.

G4 · 2257 Chestnut Street · 415/563–9727 · 24, 30

Eating with children

All but the most exclusive San Franciscan restaurants welcome children. Young diners will often be handed toys and coloring sets as soon as they sit down, and they have their own section of the menu, where child-sized portions and perennial kids' favorites such as burgers and French fries are strongly featured.

JAPANESE & SOUTHEAST ASIAN RESTAURANTS

JAPANESE

ISOBUNE ($$)
Watch the chef prepare *sushi*, then make your selection from the many little *sushi*-laden boats that float along the counter.

H5   Japan Center, Japantown   415/563–1030   2, 3, 4, 22, 38

KYO-YA ($$$)
In keeping with the luxurious ambience of this elegant hotel, Kyo-Ya serves the finest Japanese food in San Francisco; reservations are recommended.

L5   Sheraton Palace Hotel, 2 New Montgomery Street   415/392–8600   Closed on weekends   5, 6, 7, 8, 9, 21, 31, 38, 42, 45, 71   Montgomery Street

SOUTHEAST ASIAN

ANGKOR PALACE ($$)
There are less costly places to enjoy high-quality Cambodian food in San Francisco, but this is one of the few where diners remove their shoes on entering and eat their meals while seated on floor cushions.

H4   1769 Lombard Street   415/931–2830   43, 76

CHIANG MAI ($)
Friendly and very affordable outlet for Thai food; all the usual favorites and more to choose from on a lengthy menu.

E6   5020 Geary Boulevard   415/387–1299   38

THE SLANTED DOOR ($)
Good Vietnamese food, an impressive wine list, and a range of specialty China teas.

J8   584 Valencia Street   415/861–8032   26

STRAITS CAFÉ ($$)
Offers a range of dishes that mix and match various Southeast Asian cuisines; many vegetarian options and a strong choice of seafood dishes.

F6   3300 Geary Boulevard   415/668–1783   38

THAI SPICE ($)
First-class Thai food served in an airy setting puts this among the city's premier ethnic eating spots; an enormous menu includes an impressive number of vegetarian dishes.

J5   1730 Polk Street   415/775–4777   19

THAI STICK ($$)
Good-quality, centrally located Thai restaurant with all the usual favorites plus a number of house specialties, including a delicious tapioca pudding dessert.

K5   698 Post Street   415/928–7730   2, 3, 4, 76

THEP PHANOM ($)
Hot and authentic Thai cuisine.

H7   900 Waller Street   415/431–2526   6, 7, 66, 71, 73

Brunch

Brunch is a Sunday social fixture for many San Franciscans. Costing $8–$20, depending on the restaurant serving it and the combination of food and alcohol that is included in the price, brunch usually lasts from 10AM to 2PM. The restaurant sections of local newspapers and magazines have plenty of recommendations for the best brunch spots. Be sure to make a reservation before turning up.

CAFÉS

Coffee San Francisco style

San Franciscans place great importance on the quality of coffee. Cafés listed here are chosen for their food (➤ 82 for those suited to evening socializing), but most also pride themselves on the excellence of their coffee beans and serve the drink in several main forms. Besides espresso (coffee brewed at high pressure) and cappuccino (espresso topped by a creamy milk head), coffee is commonly served as *caffè latté* (espresso with steamed milk) and *caffè mocha* (espresso with chocolate).

BRAIN WASH ($)
A truly San Franciscan phenomenon: a café attached to a launderette enabling patrons to drink coffee and munch cakes while their washing is being done.
✚ K6 ✉ 1122 Folsom Street ☎ 415/861–3663 🚌 12

BUENA VISTA CAFÉ ($)
A good bet for simple, inexpensive food in a pricey area, though best known for its punch-packing Irish coffee.
✚ J3 ✉ 2765 Hyde Street ☎ 415/474–5044 🚌 32

CAFÉ BASTILLE ($)
A very effective re-creation of a stylish Parisian bistro in a Financial District alley.
✚ L5 ✉ 22 Belden Alley ☎ 415/986–5673 🚌 15

CAFÉ ISTANBUL ($)
Offers extra-strong Turkish coffee and a delicious selection of very sweet cakes and pastries.
✚ J8 ✉ 525 Valencia Street ☎ 415/863–8854 🚌 26 🚇 16th Street Mission

CAFÈ LA BOHÈME ($)
San Francisco's present-day Bohemia in the Mission District is well served by this roomy outlet for coffee, soups, and snacks—and pickup chess games.
✚ J9 ✉ 3318 24th Street ☎ 415/285–4122 🚌 14, 26, 48, 67 🚇 24th Street Mission

CAFFÈ TRIESTE ($)
Since it opened in the 1950s, Trieste has been the quintessential North Beach café, drawing writers, poets, artists, and anyone seeking a flavorful cup of coffee and a choice of tempting cakes and snacks; amateur operatic performances are staged here on Saturday afternoons.
✚ K4 ✉ 601 Vallejo Street ☎ 415/392–6739 🚌 15, 41

JAMMIN' JAVA ($)
A perfect place to begin exploring Haight-Ashbury; counter-cultural artworks are displayed alongside wholesome snacks and excellent coffee.
✚ F7 ✉ 701 Cole Street ☎ 415/668–5282 🚌 37

JUST DESSERTS ($)
One of a small San Franciscan café chain, and located usefully close to Fort Mason Culture Center (➤ 35).
✚ H3 ✉ 3735 Buchanan Street ☎ 415/922–8675 🚌 28

KAN ZAMAN ($)
An inspired addition to the city's café scene: the deep cushions, large hookahs and selection of Arabian snacks are memorable.
✚ F7 ✉ 1793 Haight Street ☎ 415/751–9656 🚌 6, 7, 33, 43, 66, 71

MARIO'S BOHEMIAN CIGAR STORE ($)
A long-established North Beach café that offers excellent *focaccia* bread snacks.
✚ K4 ✉ 566 Columbus Avenue ☎ 415/362–0536 🚌 15, 30, 41, 45

AFTERNOON TEAROOMS

BREAD & HONEY TEAROOM ($)
Tea and nibbles are served with minimal fuss in a simple setting.
➕ K5 ✉ King George Hotel, 334 Mason Street ☎ 415/781–5050 🚌 2, 3, 4, 38, 76

THE CLIFT HOTEL ($$)
A decent spread, but served in an undistinguished corner of the lobby rather than in one of the hotel's famous public rooms.
➕ K5 ✉ 495 Geary Street ☎ 415/775–4700 🚌 38

COMPASS ROSE ($$)
San Francisco's high society lines up for the privilege of enjoying a tempting selection of teas and the most delicate of sandwiches in this luxurious room.
➕ K5 ✉ Westin St. Francis Hotel, 335 Powell Street at Union Square ☎ 415/774–0167 🚌 2, 3, 4, 6, 38, 71; Powell–Hyde or Powell–Mason cable car

GARDEN COURT ($$)
The city's most ornate interior, where tea is taken to the accompaniment of a harpist.
➕ L5 ✉ Sheraton Palace Hotel, 2 New Montgomery Street ☎ 415/392–8600 🚌 5, 6, 7, 8, 9, 21, 31, 38, 42, 45, 71 🚇 Montgomery Street

LOWER BAR ($$)
Afternoon tea is a good excuse for sampling this hotel's legendary farmhouse fruitcake.
➕ K5 ✉ Mark Hopkins Intercontinental Hotel, 1 Nob Hill ☎ 415/392–3434 🚌 1; California Street cable car

MAD MAGDA'S RUSSIAN TEA ROOM ($)
A contrast to the refinement elsewhere, Magda's brings avant-garde décor and general eccentricity to the consumption of tea and scones.
➕ J6 ✉ 579 Hayes Street ☎ 415/864–7654 🚌 21

NEIMAN MARCUS ROTUNDA ($$)
Tea beneath this store's immense rotunda, dating from 1909, includes a bird's-eye view of Union Square.
➕ K5 ✉ Neiman Marcus, 150 Stockton Street ☎ 415/362–3900 🚌 38; Powell–Hyde or Powell–Mason cable car

RITZ-CARLTON ($$)
A good choice of teas, sandwiches, and feather-light cakes; the sense of decadent pleasure is heightened by a pianist.
➕ K5 ✉ 600 Stockton Street ☎ 415/296–7465 🚌 1, 30, 45; California Street cable car

STANFORD COURT HOTEL ($$)
Served in the hushed surroundings of the lobby lounge, the tea spread includes smoked salmon with *crème fraîche* on pumpernickel.
➕ K5 ✉ 905 California Street ☎ 415/989–3500 🚌 1; California Street cable car

TEA & COMPANY ($)
Here you'll find exotic brews and snacks popular with the elegant folk of Pacific Heights.
➕ H4 ✉ 2207 Fillmore Street ☎ 415/929–TEAS 🚌 45

The complete tea
Afternoon tea costs around $20 and typically offers a choice of Earl Grey, orange pekoe, Darjeeling, jasmine, lapsang souchong, oolong, peppermint, Russian caravan, or chamomile tea. This will be served with any or all of the following: sandwiches (filled with bacon, cucumber, smoked salmon, ham, egg and parsley, or English cheddar cheese), scones, and fancy pastries. Fresh Devon cream and assorted fine jams await application to your scone, but the first item to be eaten should be the palate-cleansing cucumber sandwiches.

DEPARTMENT STORES & SHOPPING CENTERS

Neiman Marcus's architecture

Neiman Marcus's 1982 opening was met with a certain sadness by San Franciscans who, whatever their feelings for the store itself, were generally not enamored of its austere postmodern design (from architects Philip Johnson and John Burgee) or the fact that it replaced the City of Paris department store building that had occupied the site since 1896. The latter's immense glass rotunda was retained, however, and can best be admired over afternoon tea in the Rotunda restaurant (➤ 69).

CROCKER GALLERIA
Designer clothing stores, food shops, and snack stands make this small, chic shopping mall in the Financial District ideal for idle browsing.
➕ L5 ✉ 50 Post Street
☎ 415/393–1505
🚍 2, 3, 4, 5, 6

EMBARCADERO CENTER
A three-level shopping complex spanning eight city blocks; pick up a free map to plot a course around the walkways, plazas, and scores of interesting stores.
➕ L4 ✉ Battery Street, between Clay and Sacramento Streets ☎ 415/772–0500
🚍 1, 41, 42

GHIRARDELLI SQUARE
A chocolate factory thoughtfully converted to house a range of entertaining stores, all with merchandise a cut above the standard tourist items found elsewhere in the neighborhood.
➕ J3 ✉ 900 North Point Street ☎ 415/775–5500
🚍 19, 42

JAPAN CENTER
From kimonos to rice cookers, Japanese arts and crafts are well represented in this complex of stores, restaurants, and offices.
➕ H5 ✉ Post Street, between Buchanan and Webster Streets ☎ 415/922–6776
🚍 2, 3, 4, 38

MACY'S
Occupying a huge site adjacent to Union Square, Macy's carries a large stock of quality clothing and much more, not least an array of edibles in the basement food emporium.
➕ K5 ✉ 120 Stockton Street
☎ 415/397–3333 🚍 2, 3, 4, 30, 38, 45

NEIMAN MARCUS
Fine china, dazzling jewelry, and racks of formal evening wear confirm Neiman Marcus as the preferred shopping stop for the wealthy.
➕ K5 ✉ 150 Stockton Street
☎ 415/362–3900 🚍 2, 3, 4, 30, 38, 45

NORDSTROM
A pianist tickles the ivories as shoppers move across this huge store's five floors, whose stock includes a massive selection of shoes.
➕ K5 ✉ San Francisco Shopping Center, 865 Market Street ☎ 415/243–8500
🚍 5, 6, 7, 8, 9, 21, 31, 66, 71
Ⓜ Powell Street

SAKS FIFTH AVENUE
Less ostentatious than its rivals, Saks offers a strong selection of clothes at prices that may not be low but are reasonable for the quality.
➕ K5 ✉ 384 Post Street
☎ 415/986–4300 🚍 2, 3, 4, 30; Powell–Hyde or Powell–Mason cable car

SAN FRANCISCO SHOPPING CENTER
An architecturally innovative home for more than 100 diverse stores.
➕ K5 ✉ 865 Market Street
☎ 415/495–5656 🚍 5, 6, 7, 8, 9, 21, 31, 66, 71 Ⓜ Powell Street

DISCOUNT OUTLETS & BARGAIN STORES

Numerous factory-outlet stores can be found in SoMa. Many leading design companies discount their damaged or discontinued lines here, and retail operations pass on some of the savings from the area's low rents. Prices are usually 20–50 percent less than in regular stores.

BASIC BROWN BEARS
Open on weekends only, this factory, which makes teddy bears and other small and soft items for children, offers its products at discounted rates and takes customers on a tour of the manufacturing process.

✚ L8 ✉ 444 De Haro Street ☎ 415/626–0781 🚍 19, 22

ESPRIT DIRECT
This huge warehouse is stocked with cartons of youthful and trendy sports and outdoor wear from the Californian design company. None of it is inexpensive, but much of it is for sale at less than half the normal retail price.

✚ M7 ✉ 499 Illinois Street ☎ 415/957–2550 🚍 15

GOLDEN RAINBOW
This is the city's largest and best discount outlet for children's clothing, up to age 7.

✚ L6 ✉ 435A Brannan Street ☎ 415/543–5191 🚍 15

GUNNE SAX
Standing elbow to elbow with bargain-seeking soon-to-be bridesmaids, you'll find clothes mostly intended for young women and emphasizing traditional styles and a feminine look.

✚ M6 ✉ 35 Stanford Stree ☎ 415/495–3326 🚍 15, 32, 42

SIX SIXTY CENTER
A varied selection from men's jackets to women's handbags, children's wear, and all manner of clothing and accessories await discovery here in the bargain outlets spread across the two floors of the Six Sixty Center.

✚ M6 ✉ 660 Third Street ☎ 415/227–0464 🚍 15, 30, 45

THRIFT TOWN
Packed from floor to ceiling with donated secondhand clothing, furniture, books, and lots more, this is one of the largest of San Francisco's thrift stores. You will find many others listed in the phone book.

✚ J8 ✉ 2101 Mission Street ☎ 415/861–1132 🚍 14, 49 🚇 16th Street Mission

YERBA BUENA SQUARE
This contains a varied collection of more than 20 outlet stores, including the Burlington Coat Outlet, which, aside from clothing, boasts a sizable selection of cut-price shoes.

✚ L6 ✉ 899 Howard Street ☎ 415/974–5136 🚍 12

SoMa revived

SoMa highlights the ever-changing nature of San Francisco. In the late 1800s, while the city's rich were building palatial homes on Nob Hill, the flatlands south of Market Street (the area known as SoMa, ➤ 51) were exclusively the domain of the laboring classes; loading rail and sea cargo continued as SoMa's staple occupation until the 1970s. As the old industries declined, many of the city's discount outlet stores moved into the neighborhood's abandoned warehouses.

ANTIQUES, ART, & COLLECTIBLES

Antique Jackson Square

An historic area with rich pickings for antique searchers, Jackson Square is a compact grouping of mostly brick-built 19th-century structures. The upper levels hold offices, while many ground floors are occupied by the 21 stores that make up the Jackson Square Art & Antiques Dealers Association (✉ 472 Jackson Street ☎ 415/296–8150). Bargains may be few, but 18th- and 19th-century European dressing tables, armchairs and chests of drawers, Turkish rugs, and fine Asian tapestries and decorative pieces are in plentiful supply.

ARTIQUES
Diverse European and American artists are represented in a stock of oil paintings, watercolors, and drawings from the 19th to the mid-20th centuries.
✚ H4 ✉ 2167 Ilnion Street
☎ 415/929–6969 🚋 41, 45

CIRCLE GALLERY
It is hard to predict what might be hanging on the walls of this highly rated gallery, but take the chance to explore inside this landmark Frank Lloyd Wright-designed building (➤ 54).
✚ K5 ✉ 140 Maiden Lane
☎ 415/989–2100
🚋 2, 3, 4, 30, 45

THE ENCHANTED CRYSTAL
Crystal and glass artfully crafted into decorative objects and jewelry.
✚ H4 ✉ 1895 Union Street
☎ 415/885–1335
🚋 41, 45

FOLK ART INTERNATIONAL AND BORETTI AMBER
Decorative items created from amber gathered in northern California sit alongside handicrafts and jewelry from Latin America and India.
✚ J3 ✉ Ghirardelli Square, 900 North Point Street
☎ 415/928–3340 🚋 19, 42

FUMIKI FINE ASIAN ARTS
Japanese *netsuke* and *obi* (the sash for a kimono), Chinese porcelain, and Korean furniture are among the exquisite Far Eastern artifacts to be found in this copiously filled shop.
✚ H4 ✉ 2001 Union Street
☎ 415/922–0573 🚋 41, 45

GUMP'S
Gump's has been held in high esteem by discerning San Franciscans since 1861; antiques come from all corners of the globe, particularly Asia, an art gallery specializes in the works of emergent artists, and another room is devoted to jade.
✚ L5 ✉ 240 Post Street
☎ 415/982–1616
🚋 2, 3, 4, 76

LANG ANTIQUES
Diverse but uniformly high-quality merchandise, spanning everything from silverware and watches to Russian artworks.
✚ K5 ✉ 323 Sutter Street
☎ 415/982–2213
🚋 2, 3, 4, 76

PARIS 1925
Admirers of art deco will adore this eye-catching stock of (mostly) art deco-inspired contemporary works and reproductions; there are usually a few authentic period pieces available, too, plus antique timepieces.
✚ H4 ✉ 1954 Union Street
☎ 415/567–1925
🚋 41, 45

Z GALLERIE
Contemporary design and elaborately framed modern posters and prints for the money-no-object householder.
✚ H4 ✉ 2071 Union Street
☎ 415/346–9000 🚋 41, 45

BOOKSTORES

A CLEAN WELL-LIGHTED PLACE FOR BOOKS
The city's leading outlet for the newest fiction, be it mainstream or avant-garde, or a selection of nonfiction (▶ 83).
➕ J6 ✉ 601 Van Ness Avenue ☎ 415/441–6670 🚌 42, 47, 49

A DIFFERENT LIGHT
Generously stocked with fiction and nonfiction titles primarily of interest to gay men, with a section of lesbian-related writing.
➕ H8 ✉ 489 Castro Street ☎ 415/431–0891 🚌 24

THE BOOKSMITH
Contains a large range of recent general titles on all subjects, plus several shelves devoted to Californian travel and San Franciscan history.
➕ G7 ✉ 1644 Haight Street ☎ 415/863–8688 🚌 6, 7, 33, 43, 66, 71

BORDERS BOOKS AND MUSIC
Local branch of growing nationwide chain stocking a massive selection of general fiction and nonfiction titles with an atmosphere conducive to browsing.
➕ K5 ✉ 400 Post Street ☎ 415/399–1633 🚌 2, 3, 4, 76

CITY LIGHTS
A bookstore inextricably linked to the 1950s Beat Generation, stocking many of the movement's definitive writings, fiction and nonfiction, and literary magazines.
➕ K4 ✉ 261 Columbus Avenue ☎ 415/362–8193 🚌 15, 41, 83

NATIONAL PARK STORE
Books, magazines, and videos devoted to wild California and the natural history of the American West.
➕ K2/3 ✉ Pier 39, Fisherman's Wharf ☎ 415/433–7221 🚌 32

SIERRA CLUB BOOKSTORE
The retail outlet of the publishing wing of the San Francisco-based Sierra Club, one of the country's leading conservation groups; the bookstore carries numerous titles on the country's wildest and most spectacular regions.
➕ J6 ✉ 85 Second Street ☎ 415/977–5600 🚌 19

TILLMAN PLACE BOOKSTORE
Small and homey with knowledgeable staff, this bookstore stocks a huge range of titles, many recent hardbacks, with a special emphasis on travel, history, and biography.
➕ K5 ✉ 8 Tillman Place ☎ 415/392–4668 🚌 15

WILLIAM K. STOUT ARCHITECTURAL BOOKS
Architectural tomes in sufficient quantity to attract both the professional architect and the interested amateur.
➕ L4 ✉ 804 Montgomery Street ☎ 415/391–6757 🚌 15, 41

Secondhand books
Besides offering plentiful outlets for new titles, San Francisco has numerous used bookstores in which dedicated bibliophiles can spend many hours of happy browsing. Recommended stops include Forever After (✉ 1475 Haight Street), with diverse fiction and nonfiction; McDonald's Bookshop (✉ 48 Turk Street), with books of all kinds and magazines dating back to the 1930s; and Book Bay (✉ Building C, Fort Mason Culture Center), where former library stock is sold at discounted prices.

CLOTHES

Clothes of unusual size

Anyone whose dimensions differ from the average can search for new clothes in San Francisco with confidence. Apparel for large and small men respectively is the business of Rochester Big And Tall (✉ 700 Mission Street) and The Short Shop (✉ 49 Kearny Street). Harper Greer (✉ 580 Fourth Street) stocks elegant items in large ladies' sizes, while Tall Etc. (✉ 61 O'Farrell Street) is for women who reach higher than most.

BANANA REPUBLIC
Noted for its predominantly lightweight, natural-fiber clothing in a range of earth tones for men and women, this outlet offers stylish, comfortable attire for contemporary urban living.
✚ K5 ✉ 256 Grant Street ☎ 415/788–3087 🚌 2, 3, 4

CHANEL BOUTIQUE
Three floors filled with clothes, cosmetics, and much more from the renowned French designer are available for the woman with refined taste.
✚ L5 ✉ 155 Maiden Lane ☎ 415/981–1550 🚌 2, 3, 4, 30, 45

DREAMWEAVER
Seekers of sweaters of distinction will find much to please here amid a wide selection of stylish, handwoven clothing. Also has a branch at 171 Maiden Lane (▶ 60).
✚ K2/3 ✉ Pier 39, Fisherman's Wharf ☎ 415/433–3571 🚌 32

EMPORIO ARMANI
Top-quality business and casual clothing for stylish men and women, offered in a classy boutique setting complete with cappuccino bar.
✚ L5 ✉ 1 Grant Avenue ☎ 415/677–9400 🚌 5, 6, 7, 8, 9, 21, 31, 38

THE HOUND
Offers high-priced, high-quality menswear, much of it based on popular perceptions of what an English country gentleman likes to wear; perfectionists can have their shirts made to measure.
✚ L5 ✉ 111 Sutter Street ☎ 415/989–0429 🚌 2, 3, 4, 76

ROLO
Many Rolo designs take their inspiration from street fashion, conjuring up expensive and extrovert attire for the daring man or woman who wishes to cut a dash on the social circuit.
✚ K7 ✉ 1301 Howard Street ☎ 415/861–1999 🚌 12

VERSUS GIANNI VERSACE
Fans of the top Italian designer can spend a few hundred rather than a few thousand dollars on the elegant (mostly women's) casual-wear items. A regular and much more expensive Versace store is around the corner at 70 Post Street.
✚ L5 ✉ Crocker Galleria, 50 Post Street ☎ 415/616–0600 🚌 2, 3, 4, 5, 6

WILKES BASHFORD
Classy clothing for men is spread across the six impressively well-stocked floors of Wilkes Bashford. The suit section offers complimentary wine or imported mineral water to refresh customers who may be dithering over those crucial decisions of what to buy.
✚ K5 ✉ 375 Sutter Street ☎ 415/986–4380 🚌 2, 3, 4, 30, 45, 76

ACCESSORIES & USED CLOTHES

AARDVARK'S ODD ARK

If looking for a choice of styles from many eras, you will be rewarded by a visit here to the pick of Haight-Ashbury's innumerable used clothing outlets.

✚ G7 ✉ 1501 Haight Street ☎ 415/621–3141 🚌 6, 7, 33, 43, 66, 71

BUFFALO EXCHANGE

If you suddenly tire of the clothes you are wearing, this is the place to trade them in and walk out dressed in something different; there is always clothing that is just in, or just out, to be picked up for a song—or for a trade-in deal.

✚ G7 ✉ 1555 Haight Street ☎ 415/431–7733 🚌 6, 7, 33, 43, 66, 71

DHARMA

Inventive, one-of-a-kind jewelry and other items fuse the counter-culture influences of Haight-Ashbury with the arts and crafts of the Third World at this establishment.

✚ G7 ✉ 1600 Haight Street ☎ 415/621–5597 🚌 6, 7, 33, 43, 66, 71

HERMÈS OF PARIS

Nothing comes cheap at this exceedingly posh outlet that features fashions from the famous French designer, but the belts, scarves, gloves, and handbags are small images of perfection.

✚ K5 ✉ 212 Stockton Street ☎ 415/391–7200 🚌 2, 3, 4, 30, 45

LA ROSA

Should a formal dinner invitation unexpectedly fall into your hands, this is the perfect spot to hire or buy evening wear that has already seen its share of social occasions; the oldest items generally date from the 1920s.

✚ F7 ✉ 1711 Haight Street ☎ 415/668–3744 🚌 6, 7, 33, 43, 66, 71

TIFFANY & CO

A branch of the revered New York jewelry outlet with more glittering stones than most people can dream about, and a dazzling display of gold and silver ornaments.

✚ K5 ✉ 350 Post Street ☎ 415/781–7000 🚌 2, 3, 4, 76

WASTELAND

Spectacular assortment of previously owned clothing, and a fruitful place to hunt down outrageous threads from the 1960s.

✚ G7 ✉ 1660 Haight Street ☎ 415/863–3150 🚌 6, 7, 33, 43, 66, 71

WORN OUT WEST

What started out fulfilling the sartorial needs of gay men in pursuit of the cowboy look has evolved into a cornucopia of high-quality western wear, from Stetson hats and snakeskin boots to exceptionally attractive bolo ties.

✚ H8 ✉ 582 Castro Street ☎ 415/431–6020 🚌 24

Markets

Though San Francisco is not known for its markets, fresh fruit, vegetables, and a small amount of seafood can be found at the Farmers' Market held at United Nations Plaza (between Civic Center and Market Street) every Wednesday and Sunday from 7AM. Avid market-goers might also like to test their mettle amid the densely packed throng on the Chinatown section of Stockton Street every weekday and Saturday when, it seems, the city's entire Chinese-American population arrives to stock up.

OFFBEAT

Chinatown shops

Exotic, entertaining, and often great value, the shops of Chinatown are among the most interesting in the city. Locals crowd the market stalls along Stockton Street, but nearby Grant Avenue holds visitor-aimed emporia stuffed with anything and everything Asian, from $500 jade ornaments to richly decorated 25¢ chopsticks. More practical but equally intriguing retailers include herbalists Che Sung Tong (✉ 729 Washington Street) and the Wok Shop (✉ 718 Grant Avenue), the latter with a good line in fearsome meat cleavers.

CANDELIER
Candles will never again seem like ordinary household objects after you view the artful and imaginative varieties sold here.
➕ L5 ✉ 60 Maiden Lane ☎ 415/989-8600 🚌 2, 3, 4, 30, 45

CLARION MUSIC CENTER
Regulars might rent a violin or cello, but casual visitors can content themselves with a stroll along the racks of weird and wonderful Asian musical instruments, which range from Burmese temple bells to Chinese egg rattles.
➕ K4 ✉ 816 Sacramento Street ☎ 415/391-1317 🚌 15, 30, 45

LEFT HAND WORLD
When San Franciscan southpaws feel oppressed by life in a largely right-handed world, they seek solace amid the corkscrews, can openers, and watches all sold here and designed for them.
➕ K2/3 ✉ Pier 39, Fisherman's Wharf ☎ 415/433-3547 🚌 32

ORION TELESCOPE CENTER
Fabulous array of telescopes to bring distant galaxies into view, plus binoculars for more earthbound viewing.
➕ H3 ✉ 3609 Buchanan Street ☎ 415/931-9966 or 800/447-1001 🚌 28

PERESTROIKA STORE
Sells a colossal collection of odd items from the former Soviet Union, from hammer-and-sickle T-shirts to elaborate tapestries.
➕ K2/3 ✉ Pier 39, Fisherman's Wharf ☎ 415/788-7043 🚌 32

PIPE DREAMS
This survivor of Haight-Ashbury's 1960s hippie days continues to cater for the needs of the adventurous smoker and anyone in search of psychedelic ephemera.
➕ G7 ✉ 1376 Haight Street ☎ 415/431-3553 🚌 6, 7, 33, 43, 66, 71

QUANTITY POSTCARDS
A small room lined floor to ceiling with postcards of every conceivable kind; the vintage images of San Francisco make amusing, inexpensive souvenirs.
➕ K4 ✉ 1441 Grant Avenue ☎ 415/986-8866 🚌 15, 30, 39, 41, 45

REVIVAL OF THE FITTEST
A glorious cache of mostly 1940s and 1950s Americana: furniture, ornaments, telephones, and all manner of quaint and curious nicknacks.
➕ F7 ✉ 1701 Haight Street ☎ 415/751-8857 🚌 6, 7, 33, 43, 66, 71

YANKEE DOODLE DANDY
Well stocked with American folk art; sort through the run-of-the-mill objects for the hidden gems, or just admire the traditionally made quilts.
➕ H4 ✉ 1974 Union Street ☎ 415/346-0346 🚌 41, 45

MISCELLANEOUS

ADOLPH GASSER
Spread across 16,000 square feet of retail space, you will find here the largest stock of photographic equipment in northern California.

⊞ L5 ✉ 181 Second Street
☎ 415/495–3852 🚌 12, 15

ALFRED DUNHILL OF LONDON
This shop goes entirely against the grain of health-conscious San Francisco, where smoking is decidedly antisocial. Tobacco devotees come here as much to admire the pipes, ashtrays, and quality cigars as to buy the products.

⊞ K5 ✉ 290 Post Street
☎ 415/781–3368
🚌 2, 3, 4, 76

ANSEL ADAMS CENTER SHOP
This photography museum and exhibition space (▶ 42) holds an extensive collection of lavishly illustrated photography-related books and other items with photographic themes.

⊞ L6 ✉ 250 Fourth Street
☎ 415/495–7000 🚌 30, 45

COMPUTOWN
San Franciscans looking for the latest software, or just computer equipment generally, swear by the quality, quantity, and low prices found here. Good for a browse to see what the wizards of Silicon Valley are up to.

⊞ K5 ✉ 710 Market Street
☎ 415/956–8696 🚌 6, 7, 8, 9, 21, 31, 38, 66, 71

FAO SCHWARZ FIFTH AVENUE
When children sleep, they dream of places like this: stuffed to the rafters with huge and imaginative toys from around the world.

⊞ K5 ✉ 48 Stockton Street
☎ 415/394–8700 🚌 30, 45

MUSEUM BOOKS
An exemplary collection of art-related books, posters, and souvenirs.

⊞ L5 ✉ San Francisco Museum of Modern Art, 151 Third Street ☎ 415/357–4035
🚌 12, 15, 30, 45, 76

RECKLESS RECORDS
Buys and sells records and CDs, and grades the used items according to their quality, promising a full refund if customers get less than they feel they paid for.

⊞ G7 ✉ 1401 Haight Street
☎ 415/431–3434 🚌 6, 7, 33, 43, 66, 71

SAN FRANCISCO OPERA SHOP
Classical music and opera CDs, records and videos, and other performing arts-related souvenir items such as posters and T-shirts.

⊞ J6 ✉ 199 Grove Avenue
☎ 415/565–6414 🚌 5, 10, 20, 21, 42, 47, 49, 60, 70, 80
🚇 Civic Center or Van Ness

TEN REN TEA COMPANY
To the delight of visiting tea *aficionados*, this Chinatown store is packed with blends from around the world.

⊞ K4 ✉ 949 Grant Avenue
☎ 415/362–0656
🚌 15, 30, 41

Coffee to go
The city's preponderance of cafés has helped make San Franciscans knowledgeable and discerning coffee drinkers. The expertise extends to the purchase of coffee for brewing at home, and the city has acquired several highly regarded outlets for what has been termed "gourmet coffee." One of the most popular is Peet's Coffee And Tea (✉ 2156 Chestnut Street and 3419 California Street), which stocks beans from around the coffee-growing world together with a formidable variety of grinders and espresso machines.

CLASSICAL MUSIC & PERFORMING ARTS

Tickets

The major ticket agency, BASS, has numerous outlets including the following: the TIX booth on Union Square (see below); Giants' Dugout (✉ Four Embarcadero Center); and The Wherehouse (✉ 30 Powell Street). For a credit card booking or recorded information ☎ 510/762–2277. TIX offers half-price day of performance tickets (cash only) for Bay Area arts events from a marked booth on the Stockton Street side of Union Square (☎ 415/433–7827).

Magic Theater

This small theater has forged an excellent reputation and stages many productions ranging from children's plays to political satire (✚ H3 ✉ Building D, Fort Mason Culture Center ☎ 415/441–8822 🚍 22, 28, 30, 47, 49).

CLUB FUGAZI

A zany revue, *Beach Blanket Babylon*, has been running for 20 years at this North Beach venue, and continues to sell out.
✚ K4 ✉ 678 Green Street ☎ 415/421–4222 🚍 15, 30, 41, 45

CURRAN THEATRE

This is one of several mainstream theaters that are grouped along Geary Street, and is the top choice for Broadway blockbusters.
✚ K5 ✉ 445 Geary Street ☎ 415/474–3800 🚍 38

GEARY THEATER

The main base of the American Conservatory Theater; the highly professional and thought-provoking productions on offer here are well regarded among knowledgeable theater-goers and critics alike.
✚ K5 ✉ 415 Geary Street ☎ 415/749–2228 🚍 38

HERBST THEATRE

The theater hosts chamber music, recitals, dance, and jazz throughout the year, and the springtime New and Unusual series from the San Francisco Symphony. The same building's smaller Green Room sees modern experimental pieces performed by San Francisco Contemporary Players.
✚ J6 ✉ War Veterans' Building, 401 Van Ness Avenue ☎ 415/392–4400 🚍 5, 10, 20, 21, 42, 47, 49, 60, 70, 80 🚇 Civic Center or Van Ness

LOUISE M. DAVIES SYMPHONY HALL

This is the home of the San Francisco Symphony orchestra, whose season runs from September to May. Their summer appearances include a Beethoven Festival, a pops series, and a special performance with the Joffrey Ballet.
✚ J6 ✉ 201 Van Ness Avenue ☎ 415/431–5400 🚍 5, 10, 20, 21, 42, 47, 49, 60, 70, 80 🚇 Van Ness or Civic Center

THEATER RHINOCEROS

The home of the U.S.A.'s first gay and lesbian theater company; the diverse offerings often explore social attitudes and behavior.
✚ J8 ✉ 2926 16th Street ☎ 415/861–5079 🚍 14, 22, 26, 33, 49 🚇 16th Street Mission

WAR MEMORIAL OPERA HOUSE

The Opera House is the venue for the San Francisco Opera's September–December season. Most tickets are sold months in advance, although a limited number of standing tickets are available two hours before a performance. The San Francisco Ballet appears at the same venue from February to May, and returns at Christmas for a performance of *Nutcracker*.
✚ J6 ✉ 301 Van Ness Avenue ☎ 415/864–3330 🚍 5, 10, 20, 21, 42, 47, 49, 60, 70, 80 🚇 Van Ness or Civic Center

ROCK, JAZZ, & BLUES SPOTS

CLUB 181
This small but stylish jazz club mostly features mainstream acts, but sometimes switches to jazz-funk or the more esoteric and experimental sounds of acid bop.
K6 181 Eddy Street
415/673–8181 19, 31
Powell Street

THE FILLMORE
This is the legendary venue of the psychedelic era, now revamped and showcasing the pick of the Bay Area and internationally known touring rock bands.
H5 1805 Geary Street
415/346–6000
38

JAZZ AT PEARL'S
This enjoyable jazz spot draws an informed and appreciative crowd, and is a likely place to catch the hottest local— and often national— names.
K4 256 Columbus Avenue 415/291–8255
41, 83

LOU'S PIER 47
The top-notch blues performers who regularly appear here draw appreciative audiences and are one of the few reasons why San Franciscans mingle with the tourist hordes at Fisherman's Wharf. It offers two shows daily.
J3 300 Jefferson Street 415/771–0377
32; Powell–Hyde cable car

RASSELAS
At this combined jazz and supper club you can savor Ethiopian food and listen to some of the better local combos.
G5 2801 California Street 415/567–5010
1, 4

THE SALOON
This spit-and-sawdust saloon, with a history that reaches back to the 1800s, makes a great backdrop for no-frills performances by rock and blues bands.
K4 1232 Grant Avenue 415/989–7666
15, 41, 45, 83

SLIM'S
The excellent sound system and convivial atmosphere make this one of the city's best club-sized music spots for quality rock, jazz, or R&B acts every night.
K7 333 Eleventh Street 415/621–3330
9, 42

UP & DOWN CLUB
The club is a comfortable and dependable location for enjoying some of the city's most promising jazz performers and the occasional rock act.
K6 1151 Folsom Street
415/626–2388 12

THE WARFIELD
A barnlike space that lacks atmosphere, but this is one of the city's major places for the biggest names in rock.
K6 982 Market Street
415/775–7722 5, 6, 7, 9, 21, 66, 71 Civic Center or Powell Street

Blues by the bay

Over a weekend each September, the San Francisco Blues Festival brings some of the genre's leading exponents to daylong open air concerts at Great Meadow, near Fort Mason Culture Center, with a Friday afternoon curtain-raising concert taking place at Justin Herman Plaza, next to the Embarcadero Center. The enjoyable and relaxed event has been taking place for more than 20 years. For ticket details
415/826–6837

Opening times

Most discos, clubs, and bars open seven nights a week, usually from around 9PM, but are busiest around midnight.

NIGHTCLUBS

Guided nightclubbing

If deciding where to strut your stuff in the San Francisco night proves impossible, you might relish the assistance of Three Babes and a Bus (☎ 415/552–CLUB), a company that will carry you—and a busload of similarly indecisive individuals—on a four-hour tour of some of the city's hottest nightspots (Fridays and Saturdays only). The $30 price includes admission and special ID allowing you to walk straight in, even when there is a line.

BAHIA CABANA
Live and recorded Brazilian beats and red-hot salsa rhythms make this the best place in the city for genuine dance enthusiasts.
✚ J7 ✉ 1600 Market Street
☎ 415/626–3306 🚌 6, 7, 66, 71 🚇 Van Ness

CESAR'S LATIN PALACE
Legendary Hispanic hot-spot for salsa, jazz, and funk: the rhythms are eagerly lapped up by a sharply dressed, hedonistic crowd.
✚ J10 ✉ 3140 Mission Street ☎ 415/648–6611
🚌 14, 49 🚇 24th Street Mission

CLUB DV8
The latest and grooviest dance sounds attract an arty and alternative crowd, as do the regular poetry readings, tattooings, and other bizarre events that take place in the side rooms.
✚ L5 ✉ 55 Natoma Street
☎ 415/777–1419 🚌 12

CLUB OZ
A wealthy and sophisticated crowd gathers to dance on this high-class hotel's 32nd floor, where the disco replicates a woodland glade in sumptuous style.
✚ K5 ✉ Westin St. Francis Hotel, 335 Powell Street at Union Square ☎ 415/774–0116
🚌 2, 3, 4, 6, 38, 71; Powell–Hyde or Powell–Mason cable car

DNA LOUNGE
A noted indie rock music venue and one where the seemingly nocturnal doyens of the city's cultural cutting edge gather to pose and strut. Depending on the night of the week, all manner of weird and wonderful avant-garde acts appear here.
✚ K7 ✉ 375 Eleventh Street
☎ 415/626–1409 🚌 9, 42

END-UP
The biggest and most dependable of a number of gay- and lesbian-oriented nightspots, with riotous dance music every night.
✚ L6 ✉ 995 Harrison Street
☎ 415/495–9550
🚌 27, 42

JOHNNY LOVE'S
Smoothly sophisticated and unrepentantly upscale, this is the nighttime haunt of San Francisco's rich and beautiful, and those who like to be seen among them.
✚ J4 ✉ 1500 Broadway
☎ 451/931–6053 🚌 83

PALLADIUM
A large and vibrant venue spinning a varied selection of fairly mainstream and always danceable sounds.
✚ L4 ✉ 1031 Kearny Street
☎ 415/434–1308 🚌 15

PARADISE LOUNGE
Multi-roomed club where the young and determinedly cool patrons can rove between dance floors, live band areas, and pool halls.
✚ K7 ✉ 1501 Folsom Street
☎ 415/861–6906 🚌 12

BARS

CARNELIAN ROOM
A stylish and upscale (evening only) bar on this landmark building's 52nd floor, with wonderful sunset views across the city.
✚ L5 ✉ Bank of America HQ, 555 California Street ☎ 415/433–7500 ▣ 15, 42; California Street cable car

GORDON BIERSCH BREWERY
Fine lagers and ales brewed on the premises make this a favorite of the Financial District's well-dressed after-work crowd; weekends are more varied and relaxed.
✚ M5 ✉ 2 Harrison Street ☎ 415/243–8246 ▣ 32, 42

LI PO
A cavelike entrance leads into the interior of this Chinatown bar, where the over-the-top décor seems less extreme after a few Chinese Tsing Tao beers.
✚ K4 ✉ 916 Grant Avenue ☎ 415/982–0072 ▣ 1, 15, 30, 45

MAXFIELD'S BAR & GRILL
Sip a cocktail in subdued surroundings and gaze at the immense Maxfield Parrish mural behind the bar.
✚ L5 ✉ Sheraton Palace Hotel, 2 New Montgomery Street ☎ 415/392–8600 ▣ 5, 6, 7, 8, 9, 21, 31, 38, 42, 45, 71

PERRY'S
Made its name as a singles bar for the affluent of Pacific Heights, but is now more a friendly neighborhood watering hole that attracts a solvent mid-30s crowd.
✚ H4 ✉ 1944 Union Street ☎ 415/922–9022 ▣ 41, 45

REDWOOD ROOM
A 1930s art deco room decorated with Gustav Klimt prints; recline in the deep armchairs and imbibe the atmosphere.
✚ K5 ✉ The Clift Hotel, 495 Geary Street ☎ 415/775–4700 ▣ 38

S. HOLMES ESQ. PUBLIC HOUSE AND DRINKING SALON
An average hotel bar improved by impressive views and an extraordinary collection of Sherlock Holmes memorabilia.
✚ K5 ✉ Holiday Inn, 480 Sutter Street ☎ 415/398–8900 ▣ 2, 3, 4, 76

SAN FRANCISCO BREWING COMPANY
Serves a selection of excellent own-brew beers and has live music several nights a week; very busy on weekday evening rush hours and Friday and Saturday nights.
✚ K4 ✉ 155 Columbus Avenue ☎ 415/434–3344 ▣ 15, 41

TORONADO
The various alternative lifestyles that are part and parcel of the Haight-Ashbury neighborhood can be observed at this lively haunt.
✚ H7 ✉ 547 Haight Street ☎ 415/863–2276 ▣ 6, 7, 66, 71

Liquor laws
Bars can legally be open at any time between 6AM and 2AM, though most choose to open their doors around 11AM and close them around midnight (later on Fridays and Saturdays). Provided they are licenced, restaurants can serve alcohol throughout their hours of business except between 2AM and 6AM. To buy or consume alcohol legally, customers must be age 21 or older. In a bar, nightclub, or restaurant, youthful-looking patrons may well be asked to show proof of their age.

CAFÉS FOR ENTERTAINMENT

Inside cafés

San Francisco is renowned for its proliferation of loosely European-style cafés, found in every neighborhood, and there is no better place to check the pulse of the city. Along with quality coffee and a selection of wholesome snacks, cafés typically provide newspapers (and sometimes books) for their customers; some are noted for their pickup chess games, others for their ambient music or computer with access to the Internet. Uninteresting cafés quickly go out of business.

CAFÉ FLORE
The affectionate nicknames applied to this energetic spot—such as Café Haircut and Café Bore—reflect its popularity among a mostly gay clientele.
H8 ✉ 2298 Market Street ☎ 415/621–8579 🚌 8, 37; J, K, L, M, N

CAFÉ PICARO
San Franciscan Bohemia is now to be found in the Mission District, which attracts a diverse assortment of aging Beats, radical writers, and avant-garde artists.
J8 ✉ 3120 16th Street ☎ 415/431–4089 🚌 22

CAFFÉ GRECO
Frequented by 20-somethings, 30-somethings, and long-time regulars of assorted ages, this is a prime place to imbibe the North Beach atmosphere with the aid of an invigorating cappuccino or espresso.
K4 ✉ 423 Columbus Avenue ☎ 415/397–6261 🚌 15, 30, 41

CAFFÈ MALVINA
A slightly austere interior is made more welcoming by large windows overlooking Washington Square.
K4 ✉ 1600 Stockton Street ☎ 415/391–1290 🚌 15, 30, 39, 41, 45,

CAFFÈ ROMA
A relative newcomer and worth visiting for its Cupid murals alone.
K4 ✉ 414 Columbus Avenue ☎ 415/391–8584 🚌 15, 30, 41, 45

THE ORBIT ROOM
Larger and more eclectic than the usual café, meriting a stop for the chrome fittings that evoke a 1940s sci-fi mood.
J7 ✉ 1900 Market Street ☎ 415/252–9525 🚌 8; F

SACRED GROUNDS
Occasional weekend live events, but always a good place to mingle among chess players and aspiring intellectuals.
F7 ✉ 2095 Hayes Street ☎ 415/387–3895 🚌 21

SINCLAIR'S PETIT CAFÉ
Despite doing much of its trade as a restaurant, this two-room café comes close to encapsulating the character of affluent and arty Russian Hill.
J4 ✉ 2164 Larkin Street ☎ 415/776–5356 🚌 19, 41, 45

TOSCA CAFÉ
Opened in 1917 and allegedly serving the first espresso in California, Tosca has opera reverberating from its jukebox and numerous celebrity regulars.
K4 ✉ 242 Columbus Avenue ☎ 415/986–9651 🚌 15, 41

VESUVIO
A legendary haunt of the original Beats, Vesuvio is still the scene of earnest debate and philosophical conversations.
K4 ✉ 255 Columbus Avenue ☎ 415/362–3370 🚌 15, 41, 83

OTHER IDEAS

A CLEAN WELL-LIGHTED PLACE FOR BOOKS
An impressive assortment of authors, local and national, show up at this bookstore for signings, readings, and talks.
➕ J6 ✉ 601 Van Ness Avenue ☎ 415/441–6670 🚌 42, 47, 49

ABOVE PARADISE
A room above the Paradise Lounge nightclub where poets, and would-be poets, can recite their latest verses to anyone who is interested; usually operates one night a week—phone for details.
➕ K7 ✉ 1501 Folsom Street ☎ 415/861–6906 🚌 12

CASTRO THEATRE
A 1920s movie palace, complete with Wurlitzer organ, which makes an atmospheric setting for a daily diet of cult and revival movies.
➕ H8 ✉ 429 Castro Street ☎ 415/612–6120 🚌 24; K, L, M

CLAY
The city's oldest continuously running movie theater, in business since 1910, and a favorite with San Franciscan film buffs as the main showcase for first-run foreign films.
➕ H5 ✉ 2261 Fillmore Street ☎ 415/346–1123 🚌 3, 22

COBB'S
Nationally known names top the bill at this popular 200-seat comedy club every night except the Monday "open mic" nights. Book in advance for the leading draws.
➕ J3 ✉ The Cannery, 2801 Leavenworth Street ☎ 415/928–4320 🚌 32

JOSIE'S CABARET AND JUICE JOINT
Well-regarded club for song, dance, and comedy, often with a gay and lesbian orientation.
➕ H8 ✉ 3583 16th Street ☎ 415/861–7933 🚌 22, 37; K, L, M

KABUKI 8
This eight-screen modernistic cinema complex in the heart of Japantown is the likeliest spot to find the latest Hollywood movies.
➕ H5 ✉ 1881 Post Street, between Buchanan and Webster Streets ☎ 415/931–9800 🚌 2, 3, 4, 38

THE MECHANICS' INSTITUTE
Monthly exhibitions, usually focusing on aspects of San Francisco history, can be enjoyed on weekly guided tours that also highlight the architecture of this 1909 *beaux-arts* building.
➕ L5 ✉ 57 Post Street ☎ 415/421–1750 🕐 Wed noon 🚌 2, 3, 4, 76

PUNCH LINE
Long-running venue for both aspiring and nationally known comedians, with a good record of giving future stars their early break.
➕ L4 ✉ 444 Battery Street ☎ 415/397–7573 🚌 41, 42

Spectator sports
The San Francisco 49ers and the San Francisco Giants both play their matches at 3Com Park, 8 miles south of the city. Some tickets for the 49ers may be available through agencies but most games sell out far in advance. Giants' tickets are more readily available through BASS Ticketmaster: ☎ 510/762–2277.

Stern Grove concerts
On Sunday afternoons from June to August, a eucalyptus-shrouded natural amphitheater at Stern Grove offers free concerts and performances ranging from classical music and opera to jazz and modern dance (➕ Off map at D10 ✉ Sloat Boulevard at 19th Avenue ☎ 415/252–6257 🚌 28).

LUXURY HOTELS

Prices

You may expect to pay the following prices per night, based (except for hostels) on two people sharing) and excluding taxes:

Luxury hotels—over $140

Moderate hotels—up to $80

Budget hotels—up to $40

Hostels—$13 per person

Hotel telephone numbers

Many hotels and some bed-and-breakfast inns can be telephoned using toll-free numbers (prefixed 800). Remember that they can usually be dialed from anywhere in the United States or Canada, although there is sometimes a different toll-free number for calls made within California (and a few may be available in California only).

84

CAMPTON PLACE
Excellently placed, with stylish rooms and impeccable service.
⊞ K5 ⊠ 40 Stockton Street ☎ 800/235–4300 (in California) or 415/781–5555 🍴 Excellent restaurant ($$/$$$) 🚍 30, 45

FAIRMONT HOTEL AND TOWER
Famous San Francisco hotel whose tower rooms afford spectacular city and bay views.
⊞ K5 ⊠ 950 Mason Street ☎ 800/527–4727 or 415/772–5000 🍴 Five restaurants 🚍 1; Powell–Hyde cable car

INN AT THE OPERA
Quiet and elegant, and a favorite of thespians and opera stars for its proximity to the performing-arts halls of Civic Center.
⊞ J6 ⊠ 333 Fulton Street ☎ 800/325–2708 (in California), 800/423–9610 (in USA), or 415/863–8400 🍴 Excellent restaurant ($$$) 🚍 5, 21

MANDARIN ORIENTAL
Sizable and opulently furnished rooms; some rooms—and bathrooms—have fabulous city views.
⊞ L5 ⊠ 222 Sansome Street ☎ 415/885–0999 🍴 Excellent restaurant ($$/$$$) 🚍 42

THE MIYAKO
Fusing the ideas of East and West, some of the rooms are designed in traditional Japanese style with tatami mats and futons.
⊞ H5 ⊠ 1625 Post Street ☎ 800/533–4567 or

415/922–3200 🍴 Excellent restaurant ($$/$$$) 🚍 2, 3, 4

THE PALACE
A stunning $60-million renovation of the city's first luxury hotel.
⊞ L5 ⊠ 2 New Montgomery Street ☎ 800/325–3535 or 415/392–8600 🍴 Three excellent restaurants (all $$$) 🚍 5, 6, 7, 8, 9, 21, 31, 38, 42, 45, 71 🚇 Montgomery Street

RITZ-CARLTON
Sumptuous rooms; on-site fitness center and swimming pool.
⊞ K5 ⊠ 600 Stockton Street ☎ 800/241–3333 or 415/296–7465 🍴 Two excellent restaurants (both $$$) 🚍 30, 45; California Street cable car

THE SHERMAN HOUSE
A lovingly restored 1870s mansion in an upscale residential area.
⊞ H4 ⊠ 2160 Green Street ☎ 415/563–3600 🍴 Excellent restaurant ($$$); breakfast included 🚍 22, 24, 41, 45

WESTIN ST. FRANCIS
A San Franciscan landmark since 1904 and resoundingly aristocratic.
⊞ K5 ⊠ 335 Powell Street at Union Square ☎ 800/228–3000 or 415/397–7000 🍴 Very good café ($$) 🚍 2, 3, 4, 6, 38, 71; Powell–Hyde or Powell–Mason cable car

WHITE SWAN INN
English antiques and furnishings enhance the low-key elegance in this 1908 building.
⊞ K5 ⊠ 845 Bush Street ☎ 415/775–1755 🍴 Breakfast and afternoon tea included 🚍 2, 3, 4, 27, 76

MID-RANGE HOTELS

ALAMO SQUARE INN
On scenic Alamo Square and offering a choice of antiques-filled or high-tech accommodations in two adjoining Victorians.
✚ H6 ✉ 719 Scott Street ☎ 800/345–9888 or 415/992–2055 🍴 Breakfast and evening wine included 🚌 21

THE ANDREWS
Small, hospitable hotel with pastel-peach color scheme, and fresh coffee, croissants, and fruit at your door each morning.
✚ K5 ✉ 624 Post Street ☎ 800/926–3739 or 415/563–6877 🍴 Breakfast included 🚌 2, 3, 4, 27, 76

ARCHBISHOP'S MANSION
Dating from 1904 and transformed from a genuine archbishop's residence to an inn with 15 antiques-filled rooms.
✚ H6 ✉ 1000 Fulton Street ☎ 800/543–5820 (in California) or 415/563–7872 🍴 Breakfast included 🚌 5, 21

HARBOR COURT
Formerly a YMCA, this cozy hotel is noted for exemplary service. Free access to YMCA facilities.
✚ M5 ✉ 165 Steuart Street ☎ 800/346–0555 or 415/882–1300 🍴 Harry Denton's Bar and Grill 🚌 30X, 32, 45

PHOENIX HOTEL
An upbeat color scheme, heated outdoor pool, and relaxed mood make this popular with visiting rock stars.
✚ J6 ✉ 601 Eddy Street ☎ 800/CITY–INN or 415/776–1380 🍴 Good

restaurant ($$); breakfast included 🚌 19, 31

THE RED VICTORIAN
The quintessential Californian experience; the guest rooms are situated above a gallery of meditative art and a wholefood café.
✚ F/G7 ✉ 1665 Haight Street ☎ 415/864–1978 🍴 Breakfast included 🚌 6, 7, 43, 66, 71

STANYAN PARK HOTEL
A small hotel with a friendly mood; adjacent to Golden Gate Park.
✚ F7 ✉ 750 Stanyan Street ☎ 415/751–1000 🍴 Breakfast included 🚌 6, 7, 33, 43, 66, 71

TRITON
With bold and arty designs throughout, this is tailor-made for the trend-conscious traveler.
✚ K5 ✉ 342 Grant Avenue ☎ 800/433–6611 or 415/394–0500 🍴 Good café ($$) 🚌 2, 3, 4, 76

VINTAGE COURT
Classy and comfortable, with rooms labeled not with numbers but with the names of selected Wine Country wineries.
✚ K5 ✉ 650 Bush Street ☎ 800/654–1100 or 415/392–4666 🍴 Excellent restaurant ($$$); complimentary evening wine 🚌 2, 3, 4, 30, 76

WASHINGTON SQUARE INN
Homey and in an ideal North Beach location.
✚ K4 ✉ 1660 Stockton Street ☎ 800/388–0220 (in California) or 415/981–4220 🍴 Breakfast and afternoon tea included 🚌 15, 30, 39, 41, 45

Bookings

Reservations should be made as early as possible, either by phone, fax, or mail. A deposit (usually by credit card) equivalent to the nightly rate will ensure your room is held at least until 6PM; if you are arriving later, inform the hotel. Credit card is the usual payment method; traveler's checks or cash can be used but payment will then be expected in advance. The total charge will include the city's 12 percent accommodations tax.

BUDGET ACCOMMODATIONS

Bed and breakfast

San Francisco's bed-and-breakfast inns, which are typically converted Victorian homes sumptuously furnished and stuffed with antiques, offer a friendly alternative to hotels. B&B owners will often attend to guests personally, serving them a healthy homecooked breakfast, and will readily pass on their knowledge of the city. Reflecting the fact that both the individual properties and the rooms within them can vary greatly, B&Bs spanning all price categories are found all over the city. Advance booking is always recommended. B&B accommodations can be arranged through: Bed & Breakfast International (✉ P.O. Box 282910, San Francisco, CA 94128-2910 ☎ 415/696-1690. Reservations: 800/872-4500); or Bed & Breakfast San Francisco (✉ P.O. Box 420009, San Francisco, CA 94142 ☎ 415/479-1913).

ADELAIDE INN
Pension with bright, clean rooms, and situated in the Financial District.
➕ K5 ✉ 5 Isadora Duncan Court (off Taylor Street, between Geary and Post Streets) ☎ 415/441-2474 or 415/441-2261 🚌 2, 3, 4, 38, 76

GRANT PLAZA
In the heart of Chinatown, offering small but nicely furnished rooms with private bathrooms.
➕ K5 ✉ 465 Grant Avenue ☎ 800/472-6899 or 415/434-3883 🚌 15, 30, 45

24 HENRY
A friendly five-room guest house in the Castro district, run by and chiefly aimed at gay men.
➕ H7 ✉ 24 Henry Street ☎ 800/900-5686 or 415/864-5686 🍴 Breakfast included 🚌 24, 37

HOSTELLING INTERNATIONAL SAN FRANCISCO FORT MASON
The largest youth hostel in the U.S., with small dormitories, laundry facilities, and a great view across the Golden Gate. Advance reservations only and a three-night limit in summer.
➕ H3 ✉ Building 240, Fort Mason ☎ 415/771-7277 🍴 Kitchens 🚌 28, 49

INTER-CLUB/GLOBE HOSTEL
Pitched at globetrotting backpackers (U.S. citizens must show evidence of recent foreign travel), this welcoming hostel has small dorms, safety deposit boxes, and no curfew.
➕ K6 ✉ 10 Hallam Place ☎ 415/431-0540 🍴 Café 🚌 12

MARINA MOTEL
Plain and simple motel on the north edge of Pacific Heights, with a choice of regular and kitchen-equipped rooms.
➕ G4 ✉ 2576 Lombard Street ☎ 800/346-6118 or 415/921-9406 🚌 28, 43, 76

MARY ELIZABETH INN
For women only, this Edwardian building with unobtrusive Methodist church connections provides a quiet base.
➕ K5 ✉ 1040 Bush Street ☎ 415/673-6768 🍴 Two daily meals included 🚌 27

SAN REMO HOTEL
A fully renovated 1906 Italianate villa between North Beach and Fisherman's Wharf, with simple but appealing rooms (few with bathrooms) grouped around a central atrium.
➕ K3 ✉ 2237 Mason Street ☎ 800/352-7365 or 415/776-8688 🚌 15, 30, 39, 41

TOWN HOUSE MOTEL
Simply furnished, well kept, and convenient to many sights. Good value.
➕ H4 ✉ 1650 Lombard Street ☎ 800/255-1516 or 415/885-5163 🍴 Continental breakfast included 🚌 76

SAN FRANCISCO's
travel facts

ARRIVING & DEPARTING

When to go

- Tourist months are July and August.
- September and October are better times to visit—the weather is warm and sunny, and the crowds have thinned.
- San Francisco's many events occur throughout the year (➤ 22).

Climate

- San Francisco's climate is generally mild. Morning and evening fogs hold the temperature down between June and August, so September and October are the city's sunniest— and most enjoyable—months.
- Bring a sweater or jacket for evening outings.
- An umbrella is always useful; most rainfall occurs between November and March.

Arriving by air

- The major gateway to San Francisco is the San Francisco International Airport (☎ 415/876–7809), just south of the city, off U.S. 101. Several domestic airlines serve the Oakland Airport (☎ 415/577–4000), which is across the bay but not much farther away from downtown San Francisco (via I-880 and I-80), although traffic on the Bay Bridge may at times make travel time longer. Flying time is five hours from New York, four hours from Chicago, and one hour from Los Angeles.
- Carriers serving San Francisco include:
  Alaska Air (☎ 800/426–0333);
  American (☎ 800/433–7300);
  Continental (☎ 800/525–0280);
  Delta (☎ 800/221–1212);
  Southwest (☎ 800/435–9792);
  TWA (☎ 800/221–2000);
  United (☎ 800/241–6522); and
  USAir (☎ 800/428–4322).
- For inexpensive, no-frills flights, contact Midwest Express (☎ 800/452–2022), based in Milwaukee, which serves 45 U.S. cities in the Midwest and on both coasts, including San Francisco.
- Privately run minibuses will pick up passengers from the traffic island directly outside the terminal.
- The SFO Airporter coach (☎ 415/495–8404) runs every 20 minutes between 5AM and 11PM from the airport to hotels around Union Square; the fare is currently $9 (round trip $15).
- Depending on traffic conditions, a taxi into the city will cost $30–$40.
- Airport information ☎ 415/761–7809. Super Shuttle ☎ 415/558–8500.
- To register complaints about charter and scheduled airlines, contact the U.S. Department of Transportation's Office of Consumer Affairs ✉ 400 7th Street NW, Washington, DC 20590 ☎ 202/366–2220 or 800/322–7873.
- An established consolidator selling to the public is TFI Tours International ✉ 34 W. 32nd Street, New York, NY 10001 ☎ 212/736–1140 or 800/745–8000.

Arriving by bus

- Greyhound buses into San Francisco terminate at the Transbay Terminal, First and Mission Streets.
- Information ☎ 800/231–2222.

Arriving by train

- Passengers disembark east of the

city at Emeryville and continue to San Francisco's Transbay Terminal by free shuttle bus.
• Information ☎ 800/872–7245.

ESSENTIAL FACTS

Travel insurance
• Travel insurance covering baggage, health, and trip cancellation or interruptions is available from:
World Access ✉ Box 90315, Richmond, VA 23286 ☎ 804/285–3300 or 800/284–8300; **Carefree Travel Insurance** ✉ Box 9366, 100 Garden City Plaza, Garden City, NY 11530 ☎ 516/294–0220 or 800/323–3149; **Near Travel Service** ✉ Box 1339, Calumet City, IL 60409 ☎ 708/868–6700 or 800/654–6700; **Travel Insured International** ✉ Box 280568, East Hartford, CT 06128 0568 ☎ 860/528–7663 or 800/243–3174; **Travel Guard International** ✉ 1145 Clark Street, Stevens Point, WI 54481 ☎ 715/345–0505 or 800/826–1300; and **Wallach & Company** ✉ 107 W. Federal Street, Box 480, Middleburg, VA 22117 ☎ 800/237–6615.

Average opening hours
• Stores: Mon–Sat 9 or 10–5 or 6. Department stores, shopping centers, and shops aimed at tourists in Fisherman's Wharf and Chinatown keep longer hours and are also open on Sundays.
• Banks: Mon–Fri 9–5:30 or 6; some branches open 9–5 on Saturdays.

Public holidays
• New Year's Day (January 1)
• Martin Luther King Day (third Monday in January)
• President's Day (third Monday in February)
• Memorial Day (third Monday in May)
• Independence Day (July 4)
• Labor Day (first Monday in September)
• Columbus Day (second Monday in October)
• Veterans' Day (November 1)
• Thanksgiving Day (fourth Thursday in November)
• Christmas Day (December 25)

Money matters
• Nearly all banks have Automatic Teller Machines (ATMs) which accept cards linked to the Cirrus or Plus networks. Before leaving home, check which network your cards are linked to, and ensure your personal identification number is valid.
• For specific Cirrus locations in the United States and Canada, ☎ 800/424–7787. For U.S. Plus locations, ☎ 800/843–7587 and enter the area code and first three digits of the number you're calling from (or of the calling area where you want an ATM).
• Credit cards are widely accepted throughout the city and are a secure alternative to cash.
• An 8.5 percent sales tax is added to marked retail prices.
• Funds can be wired via **American Express MoneyGram** (☎ 800/926–9400 from the U.S. and Canada for locations and information) or **Western Union** (☎ 800/325–6000 for agent locations or to send using MasterCard or Visa; ☎ 800/321–2923 in Canada).

Single travelers
• Single travelers, especially women traveling alone, are not unusual in San Francisco. Unwelcome

attention is not unknown,
however, and in areas such as
the Tenderloin and parts of the
Mission District and Western
Addition, lone females should be
especially cautious.

Etiquette
• Be aware of the antismoking
feeling that prevails in San
Francisco. Be sure to check
whether smoking is frowned
upon—or even illegal—before
you light up inside a building.
• Tip at least 15 percent in a
restaurant; 15–20 percent of a taxi
fare; $1 per bag to a porter.

Student travelers
• To get discounts on transportation and admissions, get the
**International Student Identity
Card** (ISIC) if you're a bona fide
student, or the **International
Youth Card** (IYC) if you're under
26. In the United States, the
ISIC and IYC cards cost $18 each
and include basic travel accident
and illness coverage, plus a toll-
free travel hot line. Apply
through the **Council on
International Educational
Exchange** (CIEE ✉ 205 E. 42nd
Street, 16th Floor, New York,
NY 10017 ☎ 212/822–2700),
with locations in Boston
(☎ 273 Newbury Street, Boston,
MA 02116 ☎ 617/266–1926),
Miami (☎ 9100 S. Dadeland
Boulevard, Miami, FL 33156
☎ 305/670–9261), Los Angeles
(✉ 10904 Lindbrook Drive,
Los Angeles, CA 90024
☎ 310/208–3551), at 43 college
towns nationwide, and in the
United Kingdom (✉ 28A Poland
Street, London W1V 3DB
☎ 0171 437 7767). Twice a year,
it publishes *Student Travels*
magazine. The CIEE's

Council Travel Service offers
domestic air passes for bargain
travel within the United States
and is the exclusive U.S. agent
for several student-discount
cards.
• Anyone aged under 21 is
forbidden to buy alcohol and may
be denied admission to some
nightclubs.

Time differences
• San Francisco is three hours
behind the east coast.

Rest rooms
• Public buildings are obliged to
provide rest rooms, which are
almost always maintained in
immaculate condition, as
are those in hotel lobbies,
restaurants, and most bars.

PUBLIC TRANSPORTATION
• Much of San Francisco can be
explored comfortably by
walking, but the city has an
excellent public transportation
system made up of buses, cable
cars, and the underground
BART system.
• MUNI (buses and cable cars)
☎ 415/673–MUNI.
• A partially underground street
car system serves the outer
neighborhoods, but it is unlikely
to be of great use to visitors.
Taxis need only be used if you
are in a rush, traveling late at
night when public transportation
services are skeletal, or to pass
quickly through unsalubrious
neighborhoods.

Cable cars
• Cable cars are more of a tourist
attraction than a practical means

of getting around, and they operate on just three routes: two (Powell–Mason and Powell–Hyde) run between Market Street and Fisherman's Wharf, and another (California Street) runs between the Financial District and Nob Hill.

- Tickets cost $2 per ride and should be bought from the self-service machines at the end of each route, or from the conductor when you board. Cable cars operate between 6AM and 1AM.

Buses
- Buses cover the entire city.
- The flat fare is currently $1; to change buses on a single ride, ask the driver for a free transfer ticket. Exact change (coins or a dollar bill) is necessary and should be fed into the machine next to the driver when boarding.
- Buses operate 5AM–1AM; outside these hours a reduced frequency service on the main routes is provided by the so-called "Owl Service" buses.

BART
- The swift and efficient Bay Area Rapid Transit (BART) system is chiefly of use for crossing the bay to Berkeley and Oakland, though it also runs through the city and forms a speedy link between the Financial District, Civic Center and the Mission District.
- Fares range from $1.05 to $3.85 according to distance traveled. Tickets can be bought from machines at BART stations.
- The BART system runs Mon–Fri 4AM–midnight; Sat 6AM–midnight; Sun 8AM–midnight.

- BART information ☎ 510/992–2278.

Schedule & map information
- Bus routes are shown in the phone book and at most bus stops. Detailed maps and time-tables are available from City Hall and, in a style more accessible for visitors (and including BART routes), from the Visitor Information Center on Hallidie Plaza.
- All BART stations display detailed maps of the BART system.

Ticket discounts
- A MUNI Passport, valid on all MUNI services (buses and cable cars) for one, three, or seven days, currently costs $6, $10, or $15 respectively. The MUNI Passport can be bought at the Visitor Information Center (✉ Hallidie Plaza), TIX Outlet (✉ Union Square facing Stockton Street), or from MUNI (✉ Room 238, 949 Presidio Avenue).

Taxis
- Taxis can be hailed in the street or from taxi stands at major hotels and at transport terminals.
- During rush hours (7–9AM and 4–6PM) and rain showers it is notoriously hard to find a free taxi cruising the streets. Average taxi fares are $1.90 for the first mile and $1.80 for each additional mile.
- Hotel receptionists will routinely order a taxi for you on request. Alternatively, you can phone one of the following firms: De Soto (☎ 415/673–1414); Luxor (☎ 415/282–4141); Veteran's (☎ 415/552–1300); or Yellow (☎ 415/626–2345).

MEDIA & COMMUNICATIONS

Telephones

- Public telephones are found in the street, in hotel lobbies, in restaurants, and in most public buildings.
- Local calls cost from 20¢.
- Calls from hotel room phones are liable to be much more expensive than those made on a public phone.
- The area code for San Francisco is 415. The code for Berkeley and Oakland is 510.

Post offices

- Most post offices are open Monday to Friday from 8AM to 6PM, and on Saturdays from 8AM to 1PM. For information ☎ 415/284–0755.

Newspapers

- San Francisco has two daily newspapers, the morning *San Francisco Chronicle* and the afternoon *San Francisco Examiner* (combined on Sundays), and two major free weekly newspapers, *SF Weekly* and *San Francisco Bay Guardian*.

Magazines

- Free tourist-aimed magazines are found in hotel lobbies; their discount coupons can save money on sightseeing and food.

Television

- Linked to national networks, the main San Francisco TV channels are:
  2 KTVU (FOX);
  4 KRON (NBC);
  5 KPIX (CBS);
  7 KGO (ABC); and
  9 KQED (PBS).

EMERGENCIES

Sensible precautions

- San Francisco is one of the country's safest cities but the Tenderloin, and parts of the Western Addition and Mission District, may seem (and may be) threatening, especially after dark. Discuss your itinerary with your hotel's reception staff to identify any potential problems.
- Do not carry easily snatched bags and cameras, or stuff your wallet into your back pocket. In a bar or restaurant, keep your belongings within sight and within reach.
- Keep valuables in the hotel's safe and never carry more money than you need. Wads of cash are seldom necessary, and it is safer to make major purchases with traveler's checks or credit cards.
- Lost traveler's checks are relatively quick and easy to replace. Keep the numbers of the checks separate from the checks themselves.
- If only in order to make an insurance claim, you should report any item stolen to the nearest police precinct (the address of which will be in the phone book). It is highly unlikely that any stolen goods will be recovered, but the police will be able to fill out the forms that your insurance company will need.

Lost property

- San Francisco International Airport ☎ 415/876–2461.
- MUNI buses or cable cars ☎ 415/923–6168.
- Otherwise call the relevant police station; the local precinct's

number will be in the phone
book.

Medical treatment

- Find a doctor or dentist by
looking under "Physicians and
Surgeons" or "Dentists" in the
Yellow Pages. Alternatively,
phone the San Francisco Medical
Society (☎ 415/561–0853) for
doctor referral or the San
Francisco Dental Society
(☎ 415/421–1435) to find a
dentist.
- Most city hospitals accept
emergency cases. Those with
well-equipped 24-hour casualty
departments are:
San Francisco General
✉ 1001 Potrero Avenue
☎ 415/206–8000; and
St. Francis Memorial Hospital
✉ 900 Hyde Street
☎ 415/353–6000.

Medicines

- Pharmacies are plentiful in
San Francisco (and listed in the
Yellow Pages under "Drugstores").
- If you are using medication
regularly, the safest course is
to bring a supply with you.
- There are several late-night
pharmacies in the city. One of
them, Walgreen, offers a
round-the-clock service at two
locations: ✉ 3201 Divisadero
Street (☎ 415/931–6417; and
✉ 498 Castro Street
☎ 415/861–6276.

Emergency telephone numbers

- Fire, police, or ambulance
☎ 911 (no money required).
- Rape Crisis Hotline
☎ 415/647–7273.
- Victims of Crime Resource
Center ☎ 800/842–8467.
- Travelers Aid ☎ 415/255–2252.

VISITOR INFORMATION

- Contact the **San Francisco
Convention and Visitor Bureau**
✉ 201 3rd Street, Suite 900,
CA 914142–9097 ☎ 415/391–2000.
The attractive 80-page *San
Francisco Book* ($2; from the
SFCVB at Box 429097) includes
up-to-date information on theater
offerings, art exhibits, sporting
events, and other special events.
- The **Redwood Empire Association
Visitor Information Center**
(✉ The Cannery,
2801 Leavenworth Street, 2nd
Floor, CA 94133 ☎ 415/543–8334)
covers San Francisco and the
surounding areas, including the
Wine Country, the redwood
groves, and northwestern
California. For $3 they will
send *The Redwood Empire Visitor's
Guide*; alternatively, you can pick
it up at their office for free.
- Convention and Visitors Bureaus
in San Francisco Bay Area
towns include:
Berkeley ✉ 1834 University
Avenue, Box 210, Berkeley,
CA 94703 ☎ 510/549–7040;
Oakland ✉ 1000 Broadway,
Suite 200, Oakland, CA 94607
☎ 510/839–9000 or 800/262–5526;
San Jose ✉ 150 W. San Carlos
Street, Suite 1000, San Jose,
CA 95110 ☎ 408/283–8833 or
800/726–5673; and **Santa
Clara** ✉ 1850 Warburton Avenue,
Santa Clara, CA 95054
☎ 408/296–7111.
- The **California Office of Tourism**
(✉ 801K Street, Suite 1600,
Sacramento, CA 95814
☎ 916/322–1397) can answer
questions about travel in the
state. You can order a free travel
package including the *Golden
California* guidebook and state
map on ☎ 800/862–2543.

INDEX

Citypack
San Francisco

FODOR'S CITYPACK SAN FRANCISCO

AUTHOR *Mick Sinclair*
CARTOGRAPHY *The Automobile Association*
                 RV Reise- und Verkehrsverlag
COVER DESIGN *Tigist Getachew, Fabrizio La Rocca*
COPY EDITOR *Beth Ingpen*
VERIFIER *Caroline Alder*
INDEXER *Marie Lorimer*
SECOND EDITION UPDATED BY *OutHouse Publishing Services*

Acknowledgments
The Automobile Association would like to thank the following photographers, picture libraries and associations for their assistance in the preparation of this book: Cartoon Art Museum 53; Rex Features Ltd 9. All remaining pictures are held in the Association's own library (AA Photo Library), with contributions from: H. Harris 38b; R. Holmes 5a, 5b, 6, 12, 13a, 16, 17, 18, 19, 20, 21, 23b, 24, 25a, 25b, 26b, 28b, 29, 30, 31a, 31b, 32, 33, 34, 35a, 35b, 36a, 36b, 37, 38a, 39, 40a, 40b, 41, 42, 43, 45a, 46, 47a, 48a, 48b, 49b, 50, 52, 54, 55, 56, 57, 58, 59, 60, 87a, 87b; B. Smith 7, 27, 49a, 51.

Color separation by Daylight Colour Art Pte Ltd, Singapore
Manufactured by Dai Nippon Printing Co. (Hong Kong) Ltd
10 9 8 7 6 5 4 3 2 1

Titles in the Citypack series
- Amsterdam • Atlanta • Berlin • Boston • Chicago • Florence • Hong Kong •
- London • Los Angeles • Miami • Montréal • New York • Paris • Prague •
- Rome • San Francisco • Tokyo • Toronto • Venice • Washington, D.C. •